Finances After 50

Finances After 50

FINANCIAL PLANNING FOR THE REST OF YOUR LIFE

Dorlene V. Shane, CFP
and the United Seniors Health Cooperative

PERENNIAL LIBRARY

Harper & Row, Publishers, New York

Cambridge, Philadelphia, San Francisco, London
Mexico City, São Paulo, Singapore, Sydney

The authors wish to thank the Insurance Information Institute for providing the list of perils covered by various insurance policies that appears on page 103.

FINANCES AFTER 50. Copyright © 1989 by Dorlene V. Shane. All rights reserved. Printed in the United States of America. No part of this book may be used or reproduced in any manner whatsoever without written permission except in the case of brief quotations embodied in critical articles and reviews. For information address Harper & Row, Publishers, Inc., 10 East 53rd Street, New York, NY 10022. Published simultaneously in Canada by Fitzhenry & Whiteside Limited, Toronto.

FIRST EDITION

Designed by Joan Greenfield

Library of Congress Cataloging-in-Publication Data

Shane, Dorlene V.
    Finances after 50 : financial planning for the rest of your life / Dorlene V. Shane, and the United Seniors Health Cooperative.
      p. cm.
    Bibliography: p.
    Includes index.
    ISBN 0-06-096231-3 (pbk.)
    1. Finance, Personal. I. United Seniors Health Cooperative
(U.S.) II. Title. III. Title: Finances after fifty.
HG179.S435 1989   88-21097
332.024—dc 19   CIP

89 90 91 92 93 DT/MPC 10 9 8 7 6 5 4 3 2 1

*To the board of directors, executives, and staff
of the United Seniors Health Cooperative, whose
ambitious goals and commitment to helping senior citizens
are making this country a better place to grow old in*

Contents

Acknowledgments

THIS BOOK WOULD NOT HAVE been possible without the commitment, expertise, and encouragement of the staff of the United Seniors Health Cooperative (USHC), the many experts in the fields of financial and life services planning who served on the Technical Advisory Committee, and the volunteers who reviewed and tested the worksheets and provided valuable suggestions.

I am grateful to the USHC for making this book possible. In particular, I would like to thank Bronwyn Belling, Director of Financial Services, who devoted a great deal of time and effort to coordinating this project; James P. Firman, President and Chief Executive Officer; Joan Hoover, Director of Consumer Health Information Programs and Services; Stuart P. Hurley, USHC member/volunteer; and other members of the USHC staff who meticulously reviewed the manuscript and provided their expert advice.

I am indebted to William L. Anthes, PhD, President of the College for Financial Planning and an outstanding leader and administrator, for suggesting that I write this book and for his assistance in reviewing the manuscript.

I would like to thank Washington, DC, attorney Ron M. Landsman for his dedication and sensitivity to the needs and concerns of the elderly, especially those faced with insurmountable health care costs. He provided most of the information on Medicaid and estate planning.

I also appreciate the advice and assistance provided by Sean M. Sweeney, PhD, and Richard Shute, Research Analysts for the United States Department of Health and Human Services; Shauna O'Neil, Director of the Salt Lake County Aging Services; and Richard Williams, Director of Public Relations of the International Association of

Financial Planners (IAFP), who provided me with the IAFP guide to personal financial planning, "Building a Capital Base," from which much of the glossary is drawn.

For their specific help on different chapters and careful review of the entire manuscript, I especially thank Anne Harvey, Director of Program and Field Services, James M. Thompson, Manager, Consumer Affairs, and Barbara Hughes, Program Specialist, of the American Association of Retired Persons (AARP); Hugh S. Hill, Vice President of Personal Financial Management for E. F. Hutton; Harry J. Lister, CFP, Senior Vice President and Director of Johnston, Lemon & Co., Inc.; and Jo Harris-Wehling, President of Financial & Tax Planning.

I'm grateful to Nancy Wallace, Director of the Fairfax County Financial Education Center, for her help in coordinating the review committee to critique the manuscript, and to the following volunteers who devoted many hours to evaluating the content and worksheets: Barbara J. Chambers, Geneva S. Folsom, Sami A. Habib, Shirley Holden, Shirley Ann Kelly, Barbara A. Krupa, Patricia Q. Larkins, John C. Leahy, financial consultant Cheryl Alston, and Arnold Zimmer, who generously shared his financial expertise.

For his help in crafting the manuscript and his constant support, I thank my dear friend and associate, Lawrence H. Caplan, MD, ChFC.

Finally, I want to thank Helen Moore of Harper & Row for her faith in this project, her editorial expertise, and her dedication to making it a useful and practical guide.

Introduction

IF YOU ARE 50 YEARS OF AGE or older and want to manage your money as effectively as possible, *Finances After 50: Financial Planning for the Rest of Your Life* is for you.

During the past century, the average life expectancy in the United States has increased about thirty years, to the current 71 years for men and 78 years for women. If it continues to grow at that pace, you can expect your life span to lengthen by two days for every week you live. While people today are enjoying longer, healthier, and more productive lives than ever before, longevity brings with it certain problems. One of these is maintaining sound health—physically, emotionally, and financially.

If you are over 50 today, it's likely that one day your earnings level will begin to decline, if it has not already. Despite revolutionary advances in medical research and health care, you are faced with the probability of increasing health care needs and the possibility of greater costs. This combination of reduced earnings and increased expenses makes sound financial planning and prudent money management essential for both your physical and emotional well-being.

Yet today's financial environment is more complex than ever before. The simple passbook savings account has been replaced by a variety of savings vehicles, each designed for specific needs and circumstances. Our tax system undergoes a massive overhaul every two or three years, necessitating changes in planning for income, expenses, and estate transfer. Within the last two decades, inflation and interest rates have doubled and then dropped by more than 60%, wreaking havoc with investment strategies. To ignore these changes is to risk more than financial loss. You owe it to yourself and those who love you to manage your money more wisely and profitably, so that you can enjoy a happier and healthier retirement, regardless of what economic changes tomorrow may bring.

This practical, self-study guide and workbook aims to help you organize and control every aspect of your financial situation—your income and expenses, your health, life and property insurance, your taxes and investments, and even the preservation of your estate. It provides you with not only the information you need to make the most of your assets, but also the tools you need to put this information to work. Each section is devoted to one topic and includes fill-in worksheets with instructions and examples you can easily follow. When you've completed the worksheets, you will have created your own unique financial plan.

What Is a Financial Plan and Why Do I Need One?

A financial plan can be compared to an automobile trip. First you decide upon your destination. Then you check your map and select the best route. You'll need to spend some time in preparation—packing and readying your car for the journey. Once you're on your way, you may encounter unforeseen detours or road hazards that require a change in your route or alteration in your plans.

The destination of your financial plan is financial security—knowing you're managing your money as well as you can. The route you select depends upon your needs and financial situation. If you've accumulated wealth during your younger years, you may want to travel first class. Otherwise, you may find a less costly trip more suited to your budget. The time you spend in preparation—organizing your financial affairs and determining how much money you have available and how much you will need—will give you the freedom to relax and enjoy your travels. Since nothing in life is certain, you must be on the lookout for obstacles—health problems, changes in the economy, unforeseen expenses—and be prepared to reroute your trip if necessary.

This book is your road map. It will help you plan your route, make preparations for your trip, avert or overcome obstacles, and ensure a safe, pleasant journey.

How to Use This Book

To begin, it's best to acquaint yourself with the landmarks and terrain you'll be covering, much as you'd study travel folders and brochures before making your travel plans. As you look through this guide, you'll see that it's divided into eleven chapters and three appendices. Each chapter contains worksheets that are essential to charting your financial plan. Some of the worksheets may only take a few minutes to complete, others longer. In some cases, you'll need to gather certain information in order to complete the worksheets, and this serves a double purpose by encouraging you to organize your records and keep them accessible.

Chapter One, for example, deals with your starting point—where you are today, financially speaking. The information required to complete Worksheets 1 and 2 includes the value of your home, your cars, and any other assets you own. Once you've gathered the data—such as appraisals and lists of securities—store copies of them in a labeled file folder so that they'll be available whenever you update your plan. Store important documents in a safe deposit box or fireproof vault.

Chapter Two examines how you got where you are today. With the help of your checkbook and bank statements, you will record your income and expenses on Worksheet 3 and compare your expenses with the national averages so that you can pinpoint trouble spots.

Chapter Three is your official road map. To ensure that you stay on the right course, Worksheets 4, 5, and 6 help you track your month-to-month financial status. If you're spending more than you can afford, you'll find out how to reduce your expenses without changing your lifestyle. You'll also learn how to lower the cost of credit.

Chapter Four concerns your financial destination and how you'll get there. If you're able to save part of your income, use Worksheet 7 to project the future growth of your assets. If you're spending more than is coming in, use Worksheet 8 to calculate how much you can afford to spend each month so that your money will outlast you. If you're nearing retirement, you'll determine which of your options suit you best.

Chapter Five is your hidden treasure map. It locates additional income sources that can be tapped if you are unable to meet expenses. Worksheet 9 explores whether you can put your home equity to work, and Worksheet 10 compares the costs of owning and renting. If you want to cut costs via a shared living arrangement, you'll be able to decide which type is best for you. You may even be able to locate additional income by qualifying for government benefits.

Chapters Six and Seven are your emergency kit for handling obstacles and hazards you may encounter along the way, including acute or chronic illness, accidents, disability, theft, or casualty. Worksheet 11 compares the costs and benefits of the health insurance policies you own or are considering buying, and Worksheets 12 and 13 evaluate the cost-effectiveness of your home and auto insurance protection. Worksheet 14 is an inventory of household, wallet, credit card, and safe deposit box contents so that you can report losses immediately and substantiate them for insurance or tax purposes.

Chapter Eight identifies ways you can lower the IRS roadblock and keep more of the money you'd otherwise pay in taxes. Worksheets 15 and 16 help you calculate your projected tax liability and tax rate. You'll also identify ways to maximize your tax deductions.

Chapter Nine protects you from changes in the economic terrain and shows you how to design an investment strategy that yields maximum safety and return. Worksheets 17 and 18 help you evaluate and choose the best savings and investment vehicles. Worksheets 19 and 20 help you create an investment portfolio that's uniquely yours. You'll also find out how to make the most of your retirement plan, select a good mutual fund, and keep track of your savings and investments.

Chapter Ten deals with the legal aspects of your journey—ownership of assets, guardianship, planning for your heirs, minimizing estate taxes. It ensures that your loved ones will continue the trip you've begun. You'll determine the best ways to hold title to your assets, consider which estate plan best suits your needs, and complete your letter of instructions, to see to it that your wishes are carried out.

Chapter Eleven makes certain that you'll continue to stay on course. As you travel, adjustments and detours may be necessary. If you need assistance in managing your money, you'll find guidelines for selecting a financial planner. To make certain that your plan remains current, a suggested schedule will remind you when updates are needed.

The Appendices contain an Investment Digest, which describes the most suitable investments for seniors, their advantages and disadvantages, and where to buy them; a glossary of financial terms; and a list of recommended reading, including books, magazines, and pamphlets that cover every aspect of financial planning.

Getting Started

At the beginning of each chapter is a list of the materials you will need to complete the worksheets in that chapter. Gather these before you start. Read through the text before you complete the worksheets, then review the filled-in worksheet examples. These are representative case studies that are designed to help you complete the worksheets correctly. Do not be concerned if they don't fit your profile—simply use them as a guide. It's a good idea to set up a schedule for completing each chapter. You may want to do one worksheet a day, for example, or complete one chapter a week. Some of the worksheets may not apply to your situation, and you may need time to think about your answers. Skip the worksheets you don't need, and give yourself time to consider your choices. You can always go back and make changes.

The most difficult part of any trip is the planning and preparation. Once you've completed the worksheets in this guide, you can relax and enjoy the journey.

Where Are You Now?

OBJECTIVE: To determine your starting point, in dollars and cents. How much have you saved? How much do you owe? What are you worth today?

WHAT YOU WILL NEED

> Calculator, pencil, eraser
>
> Most recent bank, savings and loan, credit union, mutual fund, and brokerage account statements
>
> List of U.S. Savings Bonds
>
> Most recent retirement plan (IRA, Keogh, pension plan) statements
>
> Current value of your share of any trusts or estates
>
> List of contents of safe deposit boxes (if any)
>
> Life insurance and annuity policies
>
> Current loans and mortgages outstanding (payment schedules)

Before you can move forward on your journey to financial independence, you need to locate your position on the financial roadmap—where you are today, in dollars and cents. This amount is your starting point for measuring future progress. First, you record the current value of all that you *own*—your home, car, savings, investments, and other possessions. You then subtract the value of all that you *owe*—the mortgage on your home, loans on your life insurance policy and automobile, and so on. The final figure, your *net worth*, is your financial location at this moment—your starting point for your financial journey.

If you've never completed a statement of net worth before, it's important that you understand why this first step is so necessary. There are two reasons. First, your net worth provides you with a baseline. If you are able to save money regularly, your net worth should increase steadily to reflect the growth in value of your savings. If your expenses exceed your income, your decrease in net worth will tell you how long you can expect your money to last. In either case, this information will help you adjust your saving or spending habits and ensure that you maintain a steady course. The second purpose of a net worth statement is to help you identify those assets that can be made to work harder for you—non-interest-bearing checking accounts or the equity in your home, for example—and recognize imbalances or unnecessary risks in your financial situation. Like a tune-up, this should boost your financial mileage.

Worksheet 1: Calculating Your Net Worth

On Worksheet 1, list the current or most recent value of all your assets (everything that you *own*) and liabilities (all that you *owe*) in column 1 (C1). Round off values to the nearest $100, and use estimates where necessary. If you own your home, for example, use a value that's an average of recent sale prices of similar homes in your neighborhood (check your newspaper real estate section or contact a real estate broker for an appraisal). Consider your furnishings and appliances to be worth 5% of that amount. You can value fine jewelry, antiques, and collectibles at 50% of their purchase price (if you didn't purchase the items, use the insurance appraisal value or obtain an approximate value from a dealer). Ask the lending officer at your bank for the current loan ("blue book") value of your automobile and the current value of your U.S. Savings Bonds. Obtain the values of savings, securities, and checking accounts from your most recent statements. If you are holding stocks or bonds in your safe deposit box, check your newspaper or brokerage firm for current values. These do not have to be precisely accurate—realistic estimates will do. It's important, however, that you be consistent in your valuation method each time you complete your net worth statement—once a year. If, for instance, you used newspaper real estate sale prices for setting the value on your home this year, use the same method next year. Finally, list all of your liabilities. These include the mortgage indebtedness on your home, outstanding bills and credit card balances, and all other money that you owe.

In column 3 (C3), include a brief reference or description of where or how you obtained your values, so that you can verify the numbers if necessary and can refer to them again when you prepare your next statement of net worth.

Worksheet 1 groups your assets into five categories—current, loaned, owned, personal, and other assets. The purpose of this arrangement is to help you determine whether your money is working as hard for you as it should.

Current assets refer to cash, interest-bearing savings accounts, U.S. Treasury bills, the cash value of your life insurance, and certificates of deposit that can be liquidated immediately or within a few months, if necessary, without any loss or penalty. The cash value of your life insurance policy is listed on the policy, but if you have borrowed against it, the amount will be less. Check with your insurance agent if you are unsure of the amount.

Loaned, or interest-paying, assets entail lending your money for a certain period of time, usually from one to thirty years, in return for a certain rate of interest. Certificates of deposit that mature in a year or more, government and corporate bonds, bond mutual funds and unit trusts, and mortgages you hold on others' property are examples of loaned assets. In parentheses, after each loaned asset, note the number of years until it matures.

Owned assets are exactly that—things that you own—and include stocks, stock mutual funds, real estate, precious gems, and other collectibles. Some owned assets—stocks and some types of real estate, for instance—pay a regular return in the form of quarterly dividends or monthly rental. Others, such as your personal residence, antiques, and collectibles, pay no regular return but offer the potential for increase (appreciation) in value. These tangible assets also provide what are sometimes called "living dividends"—the pleasure of ownership.

Personal assets are also things that you use and include your automobiles, furnishings, and equipment. These differ from the owned assets listed above because they're likely to depreciate (be worth less over time) rather than appreciate (increase in value with the passage of time).

The fifth category, other assets, includes those assets you're unable to identify or access immediately. The value of a trust, inheritance, or pension plan would be listed here if you didn't know how the money was invested. If you have an IRA, list it in the appropriate category; for example, under loaned assets if it's invested in long-term certificates of deposit.

Total the amounts for each of the above five categories on lines L1, L2, L3, L4, and L5, and enter the grand total of all your assets on line L6. Then calculate the percentage value of each type of asset by dividing each category total in column 1 by your total assets (L6). Enter these percentages in column 2 (C2).

After you've completed your calculations, turn to the second part of Worksheet 1 and list your liabilities—what you owe—in column 1 (C1). These are grouped into two categories—current and long-term liabilities.

Current liabilities are debts that will be paid off during the coming year. First total the bills that you'll be paying this month. Next total the charge and credit card balances that you owe, along with the amount of any other current debts that you expect to pay off in the next twelve months. Include only the current (principal) amount of the debt—don't try to figure out how much interest will be owed at a future date. The interest you earn on your current assets helps to offset your debt carrying charges.

Long-term liabilities are debts that you expect to pay off in a year or more. If you financed your automobile or took out a consumer loan to finance other purchases, list the balance you currently owe. Consult your mortgage payment (amortization) schedule for the outstanding balance owed on your home or other property.

In column 2 (C2), list the interest rate you're paying on each debt. If you've taken out a variable rate loan, list the current rate and, in parentheses, the floor and ceiling that the lender may charge.

Total the amounts of current liabilities on line L7 and of long-term liabilities on line L8, and enter the grand total of liabilities on line L9. Then subtract total liabilities from total assets and enter the amount on line L10. This figure—your net worth—is your starting point for measuring your financial progress.

WORSHEET 1	

Your Starting Point

Statement of Net Worth as of _____
DATE

ASSETS—WHAT YOU OWN

	(C1) Current Value	(C2) % of Total Assets	(C3) Description/ Source
Current Assets (cash or cash equivalents)			
Cash on hand	_____		_____
Checking accounts	_____		_____
Savings accounts	_____		_____
Money market funds	_____		_____
Certificates of deposit (coming due in less than 1 year)	_____		_____
Life insurance cash value	_____		_____
(L1) Total Current Assets	_____	_____% (C1L1/C1L6)	

Loaned Assets (interest-paying assets that come due in a year or more)			
Certificates of deposit	_____		_____
	_____		_____
Bonds or mortgages held	_____		_____
	_____		_____
Bond or mortgage mutual funds	_____		_____
	_____		_____
(L2) Total Loaned Assets	_____	_____% (C1L2/C1L6)	

Owned Assets (stocks, property, collectibles)

Common and preferred stocks   _____   _____

                                  _____   _____

Stock mutual funds   _____   _____

                                  _____   _____

Home (market value)   _____   _____

Rental property   _____   _____

Real estate limited partnerships   _____   _____

Other partnership interests   _____   _____

Business interests   _____   _____

Gold/silver/collectibles   _____   _____

(L3) Total Owned Assets   _____   _____%
                                                (C1L3/C1L6)

Personal Assets (depreciating property)

Automobiles   _____   _____

                                  _____   _____

Furnishings   _____   _____

Equipment   _____   _____

(L4) Total Personal Assets   _____   _____%
                                                (C1L4/C1L6)

Other Assets

Retirement and pension plans   _____   _____

Annuities   _____   _____

Trusts   _____   _____

Inheritances   _____   _____

(L5) Total Other Assets   _____   _____%
                                                (C1L5/C1L6)

(L6) Total Assets (L1 + L2 + L3 + L4 + L5)   _____   _____%
                                                        (C1)   (C2)

LIABILITIES—WHAT YOU OWE

	(C1) Amount	(C2) Interest Rate
Current Liabilities (debts that will be paid within a year)		
Unpaid bills	_____	_____%
Credit card balance	_____	_____%
Charge card balance	_____	_____%
(L7) Total Current Liabilities	_____	_____
Long-Term Liabilities (debts that will be paid in a year or more)		
Notes and IOUs payable	_____	_____%
Loans payable	_____	_____%
	_____	_____%
Mortgages payable	_____	_____%
	_____	_____%
Life insurance loans	_____	_____%
(L8) Total Long-Term Liabilities	_____	
(L9) Total Liabilities (L7 + L8)	_____	
(L10) Your Net Worth: Total Assets (L6) − Total Liabilities (L9)	_____	

Your Starting Point

Worksheet 2:
Analyzing Your Net Worth Statement

Worksheet 2 helps you analyze your net worth statement to determine whether your assets are being utilized in the best possible way. You need the information you gathered for Worksheet 1 to answer the questions.

WORKSHEET 2

Is Your Money Working As Hard As It Should?

1. The value of your current assets should exceed the total of three months' expenses so that if an emergency need for cash should arise you'll have a cash cushion available. Determine this amount by totaling the amount of checks and cash withdrawn during the last three months *or* multiplying last month's checks and withdrawals by three *or* dividing last year's total income by four.

Total Current Assets (L1) _____ should be more than

three months' expenses _____

Are you risking a credit crunch?   YES   NO

2. You should have no more than one month's expenses in a non-interest-bearing checking account. The rest of your current assets can be earning interest in a money market account or fund. If you allow incoming checks to lie around for days or weeks before depositing them, you're losing money. Arrange for electronic transfer of funds, whenever possible.

Is your cash loafing on the job?   YES   NO

3. How does the interest rate you're paying on current liabilities (L7, C2 on Worksheet 1)—credit or charge card balance, overdue bills—compare with the return you're earning on your current assets? Check your most recent savings account or money market fund statement for the current yield. If your borrowing costs are greater than the interest you're earning, you're wasting money, so pay off your debts as quickly as possible.

Are borrowing costs draining your bank account?   YES   NO

4. What percentage of your total assets is personal (depreciating) assets (L4 on Worksheet 1)? Personal assets such as furniture, appliances, and equipment decrease steadily in value until they finally become almost worthless. If your net worth is $100,000 or more, try to keep the value of your personal assets below 15% of your total assets. Postpone the purchase of new cars or furnishings if personal assets exceed that amount.

Total Assets (L6)   _____

×   _____.15_____

=   _____ should be more than Personal Assets (L4) _____

Do you have a case of disappearing assets?   YES   NO

5. As you get older, your investment mix should shift from owned assets to loaned assets. Owned assets—stocks, property, commodities—offer the potential for appreciation, but also the possibility of losing some or all of your money. In addition, many owned assets pay no current return and cost money to buy and sell. Loaned assets—CDs, bonds, notes, mortgages—pay you current interest, which can be used for living expenses or reinvestment, *and* you know that all of your money will be returned when the investment matures. The value of your loaned assets plus liquid assets should exceed the value of your owned investments.

Current Assets (L1)	_____		Owned Assets (L3)	_____
Loaned Assets (L2)	+ _____		Home (mkt. value)	− _____
Total Loaned	= _____ should be more than		Owned Investments	= _____

Are you taking unnecessary risks with your money?   YES   NO

6. Diversification is a safety valve that protects you from severe loss. No single asset or investment vehicle, other than your home equity (market value of home minus mortgage balance), should comprise more than 25% of your total assets. Make certain that bank and savings account balances do not exceed the federally insured limit ($100,000) for each account. Better to have several baskets to look after than none.

Total Assets (L6)   _____

Home equity   − _____

                  = _____

                  × _____ .25

                  = _____ No single loaned or owned asset (other than your home) should be worth more than this amount.

Have you put too many of your eggs in one basket?   YES   NO

7. Were you unable to locate bank and security statements? Did you find it hard to remember what you own? Do you have assets—old stock certificates, mortgages, antiques or collectibles—that you couldn't value accurately? Now is the time to gather all this information together in one place. Maintain a file or notebook for bank, brokerage, and amortization statements and other financial correspondence. Assets that are difficult to valuate are also difficult to sell at a fair price. Collectibles may net you less than 50% of the dealer's retail price, and inactively traded stocks cost more to buy and sell, so that if you have to sell, you may get only a fraction of what you paid. When you make an investment, recognize that someday you may need to get out of it.

Did you have difficulty establishing values for your assets?   YES   NO

8. When income is received, deposit it immediately in an interest-bearing account. That way, you'll be sure of keeping pace with inflation and earning a current return. Don't rush into an investment decision or worry about missing an opportunity. Take time to investigate before you invest.

Are you putting your money in the wrong place?   YES   NO

HOW DID YOU SCORE?

Count the No answers and score yourself on the following scale:

Number of Nos

7–8	Your net worth is in tip-top shape
5–6	A couple of adjustments will get you on the right track
3–4	You may be subjecting yourself to needless risks
Fewer than 3	Changing your ways will almost surely save you money

If your score is low, it's not necessary to sell your investments or completely rearrange your assets so as to put your money to work more effectively. If you've invested most of your loaned assets in thirty-year bonds, for example, don't run out and sell them. You can simply invest all future savings in shorter-term securities in order to obtain a better portfolio balance.

Getting Started With Arthur and Mary Burns

To start you off on the right track, Arthur and Mary Burns have volunteered to tell you about their financial situation. Arthur retired three years ago, at age 65, from his position as Parts Manager for Gizmo Manufacturing Company.

Arthur explained, "I knew that when I retired, the company would pay me a pension, but I also contributed the maximum each year to IRA accounts for Mary and me, so we could save on taxes and have more to live on. Since we wanted a combination of income and growth, we decided to invest half of the money in certificates of deposit and half in good quality common stocks." Mary added, "Arthur and I have never been big spenders. We enjoy a simple lifestyle and want our savings to continue to grow. After putting the children through college, we kept close tabs on our income and expenses, because we knew we'd have to live on less when Arthur retired. True, we've had to give up some luxuries in order to live within our income, but now that we've adjusted to the change, I don't miss them at all. When the children finished school, we sold our home for a profit and invested part of the proceeds in a townhouse and part in a common stock mutual fund. We invested just $5,000 in that fund, nearly ten years ago. We could have withdrawn the earnings each month, but the stockbroker who sold it to us suggested that, since we really didn't need the money, we should request that the fund reinvest our earnings to buy more shares. It seems that we made the right decision because now it's worth almost three times what we put in."

The Burnses keep $300 cash on hand and had a balance of $2,500 in a non-interest-bearing checking account on January 1, when they completed Worksheet 1. They had $700 in their passbook savings account and $7,000 in a money market fund, according to their most recent monthly statements. When Arthur was employed, he had a term life insurance policy that was paid for by Gizmo, but it was cancelled when he retired. The certificates of deposit Arthur bought with his IRA money had matured, and he had reinvested the proceeds of $8,000 in another certificate that would mature in three years. Arthur still owned the stocks he'd placed in his IRA, which were now worth $10,000, according to the prices listed in the newspaper financial section. A look at their monthly mutual fund statement revealed that the $5,000 the Burnses had invested ten years ago had increased to $14,500. They had recently had their townhouse appraised at $85,000 and calculated the value of their furnishings and appliances to be a little more than 5% of that amount—$5,000. Mary called First National's loan department to obtain the blue book value for their car, which was $7,500. Since Arthur had listed his IRA assets in the categories for loaned and owned assets, he made no entry for other assets. On

January 1, 1987, the total value of their current, loaned, owned, and personal assets was $140,500.

The Burnses then added up the bills that needed to be paid in January. They had a total of $700 plus a credit card balance of $2,100. They still owed $3,500 on the sedan they'd purchased two years before and had a $31,000 outstanding balance on their townhouse mortgage, bringing their liability total to $37,300.

They subtracted their total liabilities ($37,300) from total assets ($140,500) to detemine their starting point (net worth) of $103,200.

SAMPLE WORKSHEET 1:

The Burnses' Starting Point Statement of Net Worth

as of ___JAN 1___
DATE

ASSETS—WHAT YOU OWN

	(C1) Current Value	(C2) % of Total Assets	(C3) Description/ Source
Current Assets (cash or cash equivalents)			
Cash on hand	$300		
Checking accounts	2,500		1st Nat'l Bank
Savings accounts	700		County S+L
Money market funds	7,000		Security Money Mkt
Certificates of deposit (coming due in less than 1 year)			
Life insurance cash value			
(L1) Total Current Assets	10,500	7½ % (C1L1/C1L6)	
Loaned Assets (interest-paying assets that come due in a year or more)			
Certificates of deposit	8,000		Ferrell, Winch Broker
Bonds or mortgages held			
Bond or mortgage mutual funds			
(L2) Total Loaned Assets	8,000	5½ % (C1L2/C1L6)	
Owned Assets (stocks, property, collectibles)			
Common and preferred stocks	6,000		INV Corp (IRA)
	4,000		AZ+Z (IRA)
Stock mutual funds	14,500		Topnotch Fund

Home (market value)	85,000	Townhouse
Rental property		
Real estate limited partnerships		
Other partnership interests		
Business interests		
Gold/silver/collectibles		
(L3) Total Owned Assets	109,500	78 %
	(C1L3/C1L6)	

Personal Assets (depreciating property)

Automobiles	7,500	Sedan
Furnishings	5,000	Home
Equipment		
(L4) Total Personal Assets	12,500	9 %
	(C1L4/C1L6)	

Other Assets

Retirement and pension plans		
Annuities		
Trusts		
Inheritances		
(L5) Total Other Assets		%
	(C1L5/C1L6)	

(L6) Total Assets (L1 + L2 + L3 + L4 + L5)	140,500	100 %
	(C1)	(C2)

LIABILITIES—WHAT YOU OWE

	(C1) Amount	(C2) Interest Rate
Current Liabilities (debts that will be paid within a year)		
Unpaid bills	$ 700	%
Credit card balance	2,100	18 %
Charge card balance		%
(L7) Total Current Liabilities	2,800	18 %
Long-Term Liabilities (debts that will be paid in a year or more)		
Notes and IOUs payable		%
Loans payable	3,500	8 %
		%
Mortgages payable	31,000	9 %
		%
Life insurance loans		%
(L8) Total Long-Term Liabilities	34,500	

(L9)   Total Liabilities (L7 + L8)   37,300

(L10) Your Net Worth: Total Assets (L6) — Total Liabilities (L9) $103,200

Your Starting Point

SAMPLE WORKSHEET 2:

Is The Burnses' Money Working As Hard As It Should?

Review the explanations for each of the following questions on the worksheet you'll complete, which is on pages 9–11.

1.   Are you risking a credit crunch?   YES   ⭕NO

   Total Current Assets (L1) $10,500 should be more than

   three months' expenses   4,500

2.   Is your cash loafing on the job?   ⭕YES   NO

3.   Are borrowing costs draining your bank account?   ⭕YES   NO

4.   Do you have a case of disappearing assets?   YES   ⭕NO

   Total Assets (L6)   140,500

   $\times$ ____.15

   = 21,075 should be more than Personal Assets (L4) 12,500

5.   Are you taking unnecessary risks with your money?   ⭕YES   NO

Current Assets (L1)   10,500   Owned Assets (L3)   109,500

Loaned Assets (L2) + 12,000   Home (mkt. value)   − 85,000

Total Loaned   = 22,500 should be more than   Owned Investments = 24,500

6.   Have you put too many of your eggs in one basket?   YES   ⭕NO

Total Assets (L6)   140,500

Home equity   −   54,000

                 =   86,500

   $\times$ ____.25   No single loaned or owned asset (other than your home) should

   = 21,625 be worth more than this amount.

7.   Did you have difficulty establishing values for your assets?   YES   ⭕NO

8.   Do you worry about where to put your money?   ⭕YES   NO

HOW DID YOU SCORE?

4 nos

When the Burnses completed Worksheet 2, they were surprised to discover that they could be doing an even better job managing their money. Mary groaned, "When I think of all the money we've lost because I leave checks lying in the drawer and keep much more than is necessary in an account that doesn't pay interest. I pride myself on being frugal, and that's just wasteful. From now on, every penny will be working for us." The Burnses were also shocked to discover that one of their charge cards was imposing interest charges from the date of purchase. "We thought we wouldn't be charged interest if we made monthly payments on time," exclaimed Arthur. "Tomorrow we start shopping for a new card."

The Burnses calculated last year's income to be about $18,000, some of which they were able to save. They figured they spend an average of $1,400 a month, or $4,200 quarterly. Since their current assets are $10,500, they're not risking a credit crunch. However, they shouldn't have more than, say, $1,500 (about one month's expenses) in an account that pays no interest, so the $2,500 they have in a checking account and the $300 cash add up to $1,300 ($2,800 − $1,500) that should be earning interest for them. If their monthly expenses rise, they can always transfer money from their money market fund to their bank account. Their current credit card balance of $2,100 will cost them almost $400 in interest this year, so they should pay it off as soon as possible. Since their net worth is greater than $100,000, the value of their depreciating assets (furnishings and automobiles) is reasonable. While the Burnses stock and mutual fund investments have been profitable up to now, they also entail risk. If the stock market drops, it's almost certain that the Burnses net worth will decline also. Arthur is reluctant to sell his blue chip stocks and mutual fund shares, but he won't add to them, either. To reduce the risk of loss from changing market conditions, the Burnses will invest future savings in vehicles that guarantee safety of principal, such as certificates of deposit. The Burnses encountered no problems in obtaining the values for their assets and liabilities. Most were found in their monthly bank and investment statements and the financial section of their daily newspaper. As for the last question, Arthur remarked, "We've always worried about where to put our money, but now, for the first time, we're starting to recognize that the simplest choices are often the best."

CHAPTER 2

How Did You Get Here?

OBJECTIVE: To analyze your income and expenditures. How have you used your money? Have you been saving regularly or do you spend all that you earn?

WHAT YOU WILL NEED

    Most recent bank, savings and loan, mutual fund, and brokerage account statements

    Checking account register

    Mortgage payment (amortization) schedules

    Most recent charge and credit card statements

Your net worth statement is the result of your earning, spending, savings, and investment habits of the past. If you have a substantial net worth, it's likely that you not only earned a substantial income during your younger years, but you've exercised self-discipline in your approach to money management and made it a policy to regularly save part of what you earn. Continue to follow your lifetime rule of preserving capital, and the savings and investments you're accumulated should produce enough income for you to enjoy a worry-free retirement.

If, on the other hand, you have a relatively small net worth—$25,000 or less—because either you didn't earn enough income to allow you to save or lacked the knowledge or ability to manage your money effectively, now is the time to make some adjustments in your spending and saving habits so that you, too, can enjoy your older years.

For those of you who have accumulated a net worth above $25,000, sound money management can make the difference between enjoying some of life's luxuries or scrimping and saving to make ends meet. There's no secret to financial success—it all hinges upon having your money outlive you.

Now that you've completed your net worth statement and determined your present location on the financial roadmap, you'll need to find out how you got there and then use that information to decide where you're going. Your income and expense statement reveals how much you've earned, where your money came from, and where it's going. Just as monitoring your car's fuel consumption will help you get more miles to the gallon, so will examining your income and expense statement pinpoint problems and show you how to manage your money more profitably.

> *Worksheet 3:*
> *Calculating Average*
> *Monthly Income and*
> *Expenses*

The information you need to complete Worksheet 3 is in your checkbook, savings, and securities statements. Round out amounts to the nearest $10 and enter in the appropriate categories. Add your own categories in the blanks if you need them. Fill in the income and expense amounts for each of the last three months in the first three columns (C1, C2, and C3), total them (C4), and then divide by three to obtain a monthly average (C5). For income and expenses that occur only once or twice a year—such as taxes, service contracts, insurance payments, and bond interest—go through your records to locate the amount received or paid during the past year; then divide an annual amount by twelve or a semiannual amount by six to obtain a monthly average. If your income isn't fixed (you work part-time or at irregular intervals) or if some of your expenses vary according to season (your fuel bills are higher in the winter, for example) total the year's income and/or expenses and divide by twelve.

Expenses consist of money that is spent on something that will be used up or decline in value, rather than something that will increase in value. If you buy a car, that's an expense, because the car will probably be worth less each year. On the other hand, if you buy a house, that's not an expense, because a house is expected to appreciate in value and thus is considered an investment. Therefore, your monthly mortgage payments—which usually consist of part interest and part principal—are partly an expense (the interest) and partly an investment (the principal). You can determine the breakdown from your mortgage amortization schedule, which is provided by the mortgage holder. Similarly, if you receive mortgage payments from someone else, or own shares of a mortgage pool such as a Ginnie Mae (GNMA), record as income only the amount of interest you receive and not the principal repayment, which is a return of your own money.

Don't forget to enter cash expenses, such as bank and automatic teller withdrawals and checks you receive that are cashed rather than deposited. If you don't remember how that money was spent, list it in the "Other" column.

WORKSHEET 3

How Did You Get Here?

MONTHLY INCOME

Source of Income	(C1) Month 1	(C2) Month 2	(C3) Month 3	(C4) 3-Month Total (C1 + C2 + C3)	(C5) Monthly Average (C4/3)
Fixed Income (amounts are the same from month to month)					
Salaries (after taxes)	_____	_____	_____	_____	_____
Pension income	_____	_____	_____	_____	_____
Annuity income	_____	_____	_____	_____	_____
Social Security benefits	_____	_____	_____	_____	_____
Disability benefits	_____	_____	_____	_____	_____
(L1) Total Fixed Income					_____
Variable Income (amounts change from month to month)					
Interest					
Bank & savings accts.	_____	_____	_____	_____	_____
Money market accts.	_____	_____	_____	_____	_____
Bonds and notes	_____	_____	_____	_____	_____
Mortgage interest	_____	_____	_____	_____	_____
Dividends	_____	_____	_____	_____	_____
Rental income	_____	_____	_____	_____	_____
Gains from sales	_____	_____	_____	_____	_____
Other income	_____	_____	_____	_____	_____
_____	_____	_____	_____	_____	_____
_____	_____	_____	_____	_____	_____
(L2) Total Variable Income					_____
(L3) Total Income (L1 + L2)					_____

(C2) Monthly Amount

MONTHLY EXPENSES

Purpose of Expense	(C1) Month 1	(C2) Month 2	(C3) Month 3	(C4) 3-Month Total (C1 + C2 + C3)	(C5) Monthly Average (C4/3)
		Monthly Amount			

Fixed Expenses (occur monthly, quarterly, semiannually or annually)

Home

Rent	_____	_____	_____	_____	_____
Mortgage interest	_____	_____	_____	_____	_____
Electric	_____	_____	_____	_____	_____
Fuel	_____	_____	_____	_____	_____
Water	_____	_____	_____	_____	_____
Telephone	_____	_____	_____	_____	_____
Waste	_____	_____	_____	_____	_____
(L4) Total Home					_____

Insurance

Auto insurance	_____	_____	_____	_____	_____
Home insurance	_____	_____	_____	_____	_____
Health insurance	_____	_____	_____	_____	_____
Life insurance	_____	_____	_____	_____	_____
(L5) Total Insurance					_____

(L6) Total Fixed Expenses (L4 + L5) _____

Variable Expenses (occur with varying frequency)

(L7) Food	_____	_____	_____	_____	_____
(L8) Household (maintenance, repair/furnishings/appliances)	_____	_____	_____	_____	_____
(L9) Transportation (gas, oil, vehicles, repair, tolls)	_____	_____	_____	_____	_____
(L10) Recreation (travel, hobbies)	_____	_____	_____	_____	_____
(L11) Education (tuition, books, publications)	_____	_____	_____	_____	_____
(L12) Personal (clothing, grooming, cosmetics)	_____	_____	_____	_____	_____

MONTHLY EXPENSES *(continued)*

Purpose of Expense	(C1) Monthly Amount Month 1	(C2) Month 2	(C3) Month 3	(C4) 3-Month Total (C1 + C2 + C3)	(C5) Monthly Average (C4/3)
(L13) Health care (doctor, hospital care, drugs, medications, glasses, hearing aids)	_____	_____	_____	_____	_____
(L14) Other (donations, gifts, losses, installment and credit card interest, property taxes)	_____	_____	_____	_____	_____
_____	_____	_____	_____	_____	_____
_____	_____	_____	_____	_____	_____
_____	_____	_____	_____	_____	_____
_____	_____	_____	_____	_____	_____
_____	_____	_____	_____	_____	_____

(L15) Total Variable Expenses _____

(L16) Total Expenses (L6 + L15) _____

(L17) Net Savings (Expenses) (L3 − L16) _____

COMPARISON OF EXPENSES

Compare your expenditures with the approximate national averages shown here. These averages are based on data collected by the U.S. Department of Labor in a survey conducted in 1984. The figures represent a two-member household, ages 65–74, with gross earnings of about $17,000. In general, higher-income households tend to spend a larger percentage of income on housing and transportation. While these averages are meant to be used only as a guide, if any of your figures exceed them by 5% or more, it may be a signal that you're spending too much.

	National Average (%)	Your Average in Dollars	% of Income ($ Avg./L3)
Total Housing (L4 + L8)	30	_____	_____
Total insurance (L5)	3	_____	_____
Food (L7)	18	_____	_____
Transportation (L9)	19	_____	_____
Recreation (L10)	4	_____	_____
Education (L11)	2	_____	_____
Personal (L12)	12	_____	_____
Health care (L13)	9	_____	_____
Other (L14)	3	_____	_____

Sample: Monthly Income and Expenses of Arthur and Mary Burns

The Burnses recorded Arthur's $300 monthly pension benefit and their $950 monthly Social Security benefit under the heading of fixed income. Variable income included interest on their savings account and money market fund as well as the interest and dividends earned on their IRA and mutual fund shares. Total monthly income from all sources totaled $1,470.

They obtained the monthly mortgage interest figure of $210 from their mortgage amortization schedule and divided the total amount of last year's electric and fuel bills by twelve to arrive at a realistic monthly average. They divided their quarterly $30 waste bill by three, which equals $10 a month. The Burnses pay their insurance premiums annually, so they divided their yearly premiums by twelve to calculate the monthly average. They obtained the figures for variable expenses from their checkbook. While some of these—household and personal expenses, for example—seemed to vary widely from month to month, the Burnses felt that the overall monthly average was representative of their spending habits. Mary Burns, after completing this worksheet, commented, "I've found that I can go for days without a penny in my pocket and I'm not even tempted to buy anything. But whenever I cash a check, the money disappears before I know it, and I usually can't remember what I spent it on." Mary felt a bit guilty about having so much in the "Other" category and determined to keep closer tabs on her cash expenditures. After they added total fixed expenses ($532) to total variable expenses ($847), they were pleased to discover that they were saving $91 a month ($1,470 − $1,379), or 6% of their income.

The Burnses then transferred their monthly average figures to the comparison column ("Your Average in Dollars"). They converted the dollar amounts to percentages by dividing each dollar amount by total monthly income ($1,470). [If your calculator has a memory function, simply enter your monthly income in the memory (M+) and divide each monthly figure by "memory recall"(MR)].

Arthur had been concerned for some time that they were paying too much for insurance premiums. When he discovered that his percentage of insurance expense was higher than the national average, he decided that it was time to do something about it. After completing Chapters Six and Seven, he was able to reduce those premiums by 30%. "Now," said Arthur, "we have even better insurance protection than we had before, and it's costing us less."

Are you wasting money on unnecessary insurance? Is your cash slipping away without your realizing it? Are you spending too much on housing, food, transportation, or taxes? You'll find out how to lower the cost of every one of these in the next chapters.

SAMPLE WORKSHEET 3:

How Did the Burnses Get Here?

MONTHLY INCOME

Source of Income	(C1) Month 1	(C2) Month 2	(C3) Month 3	(C4) 3-Month Total (C1+C2+C3)	(C5) Monthly Average (C4/3)
Fixed Income (amounts are the same from month to month)					
Salaries (after taxes)					
Pension income	300	300	300	900	300
Annuity income					
Social Security benefits	950	950	950	2,850	950
Disability benefits					
(L1) Total Fixed Income					1,250
Variable Income (amounts change from month to month)					
Interest					
Bank & savings accts.	5	8	7	20	7
Money market accts.	40	30	28	98	33
Bonds and notes	70	70	70	210	70
Mortgage interest					
Dividends	110	90	130	330	110
Rental income					
Gains from sales					
Other income					
(L2) Total Variable Income					220
(L3) Total Income (L1+L2)					1,470

MONTHLY EXPENSES

Purpose of Expense	(C1) Monthly Amount Month 1	(C2) Monthly Amount Month 2	(C3) Month 3	(C4) 3-Month Total (C1 + C2 + C3)	(C5) Monthly Average (C4/3)
Fixed Expenses (occur monthly, quarterly, semiannually or annually)					
Home					
Rent					
Mortgage interest	210	210	210	630	210
Electric	80	80	80	240	80
Fuel	20	20	20	60	20
Water	10	10	10	30	10
Telephone	20	30	20	70	23
Waste	30	—	—	30	10
(L4) Total Home					353
Insurance					
Auto insurance 1,000 yr					83
Home insurance 450 yr					38
Health insurance 700 yr					58
Life insurance					
(L5) Total Insurance					179
(L6) Total Fixed Expenses (L4 + L5)					532
Variable Expenses (occur with varying frequency)					
(L7) Food	150	200	230	580	194
(L8) Household (maintenance, repair/furnishings/appliances)	40	90	150	280	93
(L9) Transportation (gas, oil, vehicles, repair, tolls)	270	260	250	780	260
(L10) Recreation (travel, hobbies)	70	20	40	130	43
(L11) Education (tuition, books, publications)	10	15	20	45	15
(L12) Personal (clothing, grooming, cosmetics)	50	120	80	250	83
(L13) Health care (doctor, hospital care, drugs, medications, glasses, hearing aids)	40	80	70	190	63
(L14) Other (donations, gifts, losses, installment and credit card interest, property taxes)	130	70	90	290	96
(L15) Total Variable Expenses					847

MONTHLY EXPENSES *(continued)*

(L16) Total Expenses (L6 + L15)   1,329

(L17) Net Savings (Expenses) (L3 − L16)   91

HOW DO THE BURNSES' EXPENSES COMPARE TO THE NATIONAL AVERAGES?

Compare your expenditures with the approximate national averages shown here. These averages are based on data collected by the U.S. Department of Labor in a survey conducted in 1984. The figures represent a two-member household, ages 65–74, with gross earnings of about $17,000. In general, higher-income households tend to spend a larger percentage of income on housing and transportation. While these averages are meant to be used only as a guide, if any of your figures exceed them by 5% or more, it may be a signal that you're spending too much.

	National Average (%)	Your Average in Dollars	% of Income ($ Avg./L3)
Total Housing (L4 + L8)	30	$ 446	30
Total insurance (L5)	3	179	12
Food (L7)	18	194	13
Transportation (L9)	19	260	18
Recreation (L10)	4	43	3
Education (L11)	2	15	1
Personal (L12)	12	83	6
Health care (L13)	9	63	4
Other (L14)	3	200	14

Take Control of Your Money

OBJECTIVE: To begin keeping track of monthly income and expenses. How can you be certain of living within your income? What can you do to reduce living costs?

WHAT YOU WILL NEED

Same as for Chapter Two

Sound money management is not an art or science, nor does it require any unique mental facility or special talent. We all know people who manage well on relatively small earnings and others who can't manage at all, no matter how much they earn. Sound money management is a healthy habit, much like fastening your seat belt or washing your hands before you eat. It must be practiced regularly to become a natural part of your daily routine. People of any age can learn to manage their money—if they're willing to spend some time each week keeping track of their finances. Like any new activity, it will require more effort in the beginning. But soon it will take you less and less time and, very shortly, become a habit.

The equipment you require to control your finances and establish sound money management habits is in this chapter. Worksheets 4 and 5 provide a place to record your actual monthly income and expenditures so that you can quickly recognize and correct faulty financial practices. Worksheet 6 provides a running month-to-month total of how much you save, or spend, so that you'll be able to stay on course.

Worksheets 4 and 5: Calculating Actual Monthly Income and Expenses

Starting with the current month, enter the figures for income and expenses on worksheets 4 and 5, rounding numbers to the nearest $1.

On Worksheet 4, enter the appropriate amount for each category of income in the spaces provided. If you hold any mortgages or GNMA pools, remember that only the monthly interest you receive is considered income—the principal portion is return of your own money. At the end of the month, total the amounts in the column headed "Monthly Total."

Now use Worksheet 5 to enter all expenses under the appropriate categories. If you write checks for cash, make automatic teller withdrawals, or cash checks you receive rather than depositing them, note these amounts under "Miscellaneous" (C22). If you have expenses that don't fit any category, list them in the "Other" columns (identify them, if possible). As explained in Chapter Two, your mortgage expense is not the total payment, just the amount of interest paid. You can obtain this figure from your amortization schedule. If you're employed, your Social Security payment is the amount deducted from your paycheck (it's listed on the check stub). At the end of the month, total each column. Then total columns 1 through 11 (C1–C11) and enter the amount in C12. Total columns 13 through 23 (C13–C23) and enter the amount in C24. Finally, enter the Total Monthly Expenses in the space provided at the bottom of Worksheet 5.

WORKSHEET 4

Your Monthly Income

Month _____

Description and Amounts	Monthly Total
Social Security benefits	_____
Disability benefits	_____
Pensions	_____
Annuities	_____
Rents/royalties	_____
Salaries & earnings	_____

_____   _____

_____   _____

Interest _____

_____   _____   _____

_____   _____   _____

Dividends _____

_____   _____   _____

_____   _____   _____

Profits from sales of assets _____

_____   _____   _____

Other _____

_____   _____   _____

_____   _____   _____

_____   _____   _____

_____   _____   _____

Total Monthly Income _____

WORKSHEET 5

Your Monthly Expenses

Month _____

MONTHLY, QUARTERLY, SEMIANNUAL, OR ANNUAL EXPENSES

(C1) Mortg. Int. or Rent	(C2) Electric	(C3) Fuel	(C4) Water	(C5) Telephone	(C6) Waste

(C7) Home Insurance	(C8) Auto Insurance	(C9) Health Insurance	(C10) Loan Repayments	(C11) Other	(C12) TOTAL

FREQUENT EXPENSES

(C13) Food/ Groceries	(C14) Household	(C15) Transportation	(C16) Recreation	(C17) Education	(C18) Personal

Totals

(C19) Health Care	(C20) Taxes	(C21) Gifts/ Donations	(C22) Miscellaneous	(C23) Other	(C24) TOTAL

Totals

Total Monthly Expenses (C12 + C24) _____

*Worksheet 6:
How Much Are You Saving
(Spending)?*

Whether you are building savings or depleting capital, Worksheet 6 will help you keep track of your progress for the next twelve months and alert you to the need for adjustments if you're spending more than you can afford.

WORKSHEET 6

Are You Staying on Course?

Complete lines 1 through 4 (L1–L4) by entering the monthly figures from Worksheets 3, 4, and 5. Each month, enter the cumulative total (L6) by adding this month's extra savings or deficit (L5) to the preceding month's cumulative total. During those months that you've incurred a large number or amount of expenses, L5 will be a negative number (your total monthly savings will be less than your projected monthly savings) and you'll need to subtract it from the previous month's cumulative total. Don't worry about an occasional "down" month unless it becomes a regular pattern and starts reducing your net worth. Frequent down months may result in your running out of capital. Chapter Four will help you calculate how long your money will last, and Chapter Five will help you find other sources of income if you run out of capital.

	Jan.	Feb.	Mar.	Apr.
(L1) Total Monthly Income (from Worksheet 4)				
(L2) Total Monthly Expenses (from Worksheet 5)				
(L3) Total Monthly Savings or Deficit (L1 – L2)				
(L4) Projected Monthly Savings or Deficit (from Worksheet 3, L17, C5)				
(L5) Extra Savings or Deficit (L3 – L4)				
(L6) Cumulative Total				

May	Jun.	Jul.	Aug.	Sep.	Oct.	Nov.	Dec.	TOTAL

> *How Can You Clamp Down
> on Unnecessary Expenses?*

Wise use of money is a challenge to every consumer, regardless of income. Smart shoppers can trim their living costs 10% to 20% or more, without changing their lifestyle or settling for less. The following cost-saving suggestions are meant to help you rethink your spending habits and the use you make of your purchases.

Food Costs

How much should you spend on food each week? It depends on where you shop, how carefully you plan and buy, and how many meals you prepare from scratch. According to U.S. Department of Agriculture estimates, an older couple with earnings of between $15,000 and $20,000 can expect to spend between $150 and $250 a month for a nutritious diet, if all meals are eaten at home (an older single person with the same income will spend $85 to $125 a month). If you're spending more (and even if you're not), consider these questions.

1. Do you plan meals in advance and make a list before you shop? _____

Advance planning will save you both time and money. If you make a complete list of the week's meals, you'll shop less often and be less tempted to buy on impulse. List items in the order of your grocery's aisles so that you find the items you need without having to search for them. The more time you spend shopping, the more money you'll spend as well.

2. Do you shop for food *after* you've eaten? _____

Most people prefer to shop when their hunger pangs make the task more appetizing, but they'll wind up spending more than if their stomachs were full. You'll save money if you make it a policy to shop after meals.

3. Do you clip coupons and plan meals around weekly specials? _____

Studies indicate that cents-off coupons can reduce your food bill by at least 10%, if you use them to purchase items that you normally use. Look for them in the mail, in your newspaper, and on the packages you buy. Take advantage of special sale items and stock up on bargains, particularly non-perishables such as paper products and canned goods, if you have storage space.

4. Do you comparison shop? _____

Most markets provide unit pricing labels so that you can find the best buy among various container sizes and brands. Try lower-priced generic and store brands—you may find them as tasty as more expensive brands. You'll also save money by comparing the costs of fresh, canned, and frozen fruits and vegetables (frozen are generally the most expensive). When buying meat, fish, and poultry, compare the *cost of the amount that's edible,* not the cost per pound. For example, three pounds of chicken breasts (with ribs) at 60 cents a pound is a better buy than a three-pound chicken selling for 45 cents a pound. As a rule, if you count three ounces of cooked lean meat as a serving, you will get three to four servings per pound from items with little fat and bone (flank steak, liver), two to three servings per pound from items with a medium amount of fat and bone (ham, poultry), and one to two servings per pound from items with much fat and bone (rib chops, chicken wings).

5. Do you make your own convenience foods? _____

Convenience foods are usually more expensive than those made from scratch, but there are exceptions. Frozen orange juice concentrate and french fries are usually good buys. When you have the time, prepare extra quantities of spaghetti sauce, casseroles, and other dishes that you can freeze in serving-size portions and reheat later. The most expensive convenience foods are those you eat out. A restaurant meal, on average, costs more than twice as much as a meal prepared at home.

6. Do you avoid waste? _____

Limit the purchase of perishables—fresh vegetables and fruits—to what you'll use. Freeze leftovers or add to other ingredients to make efficient use of large cuts of meat and poultry.

7. Do you use a meat alternative at least once a week? _____

Dry beans and peas, peanut butter, eggs, and canned tuna provide the same nutrients found in meat, at a lower cost. When you serve meat, use smaller portions and fill in meals with more economical potatoes, rice, and enriched breads and noodles.

Housing and Home Maintenance Costs

These expenses absorb the largest percentage of your income. It's likely that some of the following suggestions will save you money.

1.   Can you fix it yourself?   _____

Many high schools and colleges offer home repair and maintenance courses at little or no cost. Learning how to paint, repair, or replace it yourself will surely reduce your home maintenance expenses.

2.   Can you lower your electric and fuel bill?   _____

According to the U.S. Department of Energy, 70% of your electric and fuel bill pays for heating and cooling your home, 20% pays for heating water, and 10% pays for cooking, lighting, and running small appliances. Keep home energy costs under control. In winter, set furnaces at 65 degrees during the day, lower at night. In summer, set air conditioners at 78 degrees or higher. Set water heater at 120 degrees.

3.   Are you buying a new washing machine or other appliance?   _____

Purchase energy-efficient appliances that have few settings and controls. They get the job done just as well, cost less, and require fewer repairs. Consult *Consumer Reports* at your library, and shop prices before you buy.

4.   Are you considering buying a service contract?   _____

Check with your Better Business Bureau before buying service contracts or warranties. Nearly new appliances are not likely to need repair, and your contract is only as good as the dealer who issues it.

Transportation Costs

Transportation costs absorb the second largest percentage of your income. If you're considering the purchase of a car, don't be lured by low-interest financing deals. Compare the cost of paying cash and financing through your bank with the best financing arrangement the dealer has to offer.

1.   Do you travel more frequently than necessary?   _____

During the next month, keep a log of how many automobile trips you make each week, how far you travel (round-trip mileage), and the purpose of each trip. Then review to see how many of those trips were really necessary. Could you have consolidated errands to save gas and time? Short trips drastically reduce gas mileage—a car that normally gets 20 miles a gallon may only get 4 miles a gallon on a trip of 5 miles or less.

2.   Can you get along just as well without a car?   _____

While an automobile is a convenience, the costs of ownership may far exceed the cost of buses or taxis, particularly if you live in a city where public transportation is readily available and senior citizen discounts are in effect. Fill in the following blanks to compare costs.

Automobile		Public Transportation	
Annual depreciation (ask your car dealer)	_____	Number of round trips per week	_____
Insurance	+ _____	Cost of round-trip fare	× _____
License tag	+ _____	Weekly cost	= _____
Inspection fees	+ _____	Number of weeks in year	× ___52___
Financing costs	+ _____	Total Annual Cost	= _____
Gasoline & oil	+ _____		
Maintenance & repair	+ _____		
Total Annual Cost	= _____		

Even if public transportation costs more, it will still save you money, because you can invest the proceeds from the sale of your car to offset your expense.

Health, Personal Care, Education, and Recreation Costs

Senior citizens are the fastest growing segment of the population, growing twice as fast as any other age group. Consequently, many companies and professional people are anxious to attract your business. Before you buy, check Southwestern Bell Corporation's Silver Pages, a nationally marketed discount directory for seniors.

1. Do you request generic drugs and medications?   _____
   Ask your doctor to prescribe generic medications. They have the same composition but cost less than name brands.

2. Do you check out thrift shops for bargains?   _____
   You can buy quality merchandise at a fraction of its original cost. Many second-hand stores require that items of clothing be dry-cleaned and in like-new condition before accepting them for resale. Flea markets and garage sales are another good source for bargain merchandise.

3. Do you stick to the basics for personal care items?   _____
   Fancy packaging and foreign-sounding names can multiply the cost of cosmetics, shampoos, lotions, colognes, and other personal care items manyfold. Low-cost products will perform just as well.

4. Do you give homemade rather than store-bought gifts? _____

Gift-giving occasions such as family birthdays and Christmas can ravage any budget. Homemade goodies, crafts, or the offer of a personal service can cost little or nothing and have more meaning than a store-bought present.

5. Do you pool your resources with friends and relatives? _____

Companies benefit from economies of scale, so why shouldn't you? Consider joining or forming a food co-op so you can take advantage of quantity discounts. Exchange a service you can provide (car-pooling or repair work, for example) for something a friend can offer.

6. Do you visit your public library? _____

Your library is more than just a book repository. It offers a wide selection of current magazines and newspapers, as well as records and tapes. Many libraries also sponsor free lectures, movies, and entertainment.

Perhaps these suggestions will trigger other money-saving ideas that will enable you to stretch your dollars without sacrificing your lifestyle. As you put them to work, you'll want to see the difference they make in your future pattern of income and expenses.

Sample: Keeping Track

For Arthur and Mary Burns, this chapter meant peace of mind. "Even though we've tried to be frugal, we realized that we were spending more than we should. Part of the problem was not keeping track," explained Arthur. "We tried budgeting, but that didn't work. As soon as an unforeseen expense came along, the budget went out the window." Mary added, "This method allows us to adjust our spending to our circumstances each month. It's the total amount that matters. If our electric bills run high one month, we know we have to cut back on other expenses. We don't worry about money so much any more, because now we're in control."

The Burnses went over the entries in their checking account, bank, and securities statement for the month of March and entered each amount, rounded to the nearest $1, in the appropriate category.

SAMPLE WORKSHEET 4:

The Burnses' Monthly Income

Month ___MARCH___

Description and Amounts			Monthly Total
Social Security benefits			950
Disability benefits			
Pensions			300
Annuities			
Rents/royalties			
Salaries & earnings			
_____	_____		
_____	_____		105
Interest			
7	70	_____	
28	_____	_____	
Dividends			130
_____	_____	_____	
_____	_____	_____	
Profits from sales of assets			_____
_____	_____	_____	
Other			_____
_____	_____	_____	
_____	_____	_____	
Total Monthly Income			1,485

SAMPLE WORKSHEET 5:

The Burnses' Monthly Expenses

Month ___MARCH___

MONTHLY, QUARTERLY, SEMIANNUAL, OR ANNUAL EXPENSES

(C1) Mortg. Int. or Rent	(C2) Electric	(C3) Fuel	(C4) Water	(C5) Telephone	(C6) Waste
210	65	15	12	24	

(C7) Home Insurance	(C8) Auto Insurance	(C9) Health Insurance	(C10) Loan Repayments	(C11) Other	(C12) TOTAL
		58	30		414

FREQUENT EXPENSES

(C13) Food/ Groceries	(C14) Household	(C15) Transportation	(C16) Recreation	(C17) Education	(C18) Personal
58	35	180	40	15	65
60	35	20		5	5
45	20	15			10
67	60	35			
Totals 230	150	250		20	80

(C19) Health Care	(C20) Taxes	(C21) Gifts/ Donations	(C22) Miscellaneous	(C23) Other	(C24) TOTAL
45		20	70		
25					
Totals 70		20	70		930

Total Monthly Expenses (C12 + C24)   1,344

Since their home and auto insurance premium is due bimonthly, they made no payment in March. They added the expenses that recur monthly or less frequently ($414) to those that occur frequently or randomly ($930) to obtain a total expense figure for the month ($1,344). They then entered these amounts, along with the previous two months' approximate income and expenses from Worksheet 3, on Worksheet 6.

In the future, all of the figures on Worksheet 6 will be transferred each month as the Burnses recalculate income and expenses on Worksheets 4 and 5. In January, they were able to save $287, which was $196 more than their savings projection on Worksheet 3 (L17). However, because they paid their automobile and home insurance premiums in February, they saved only $27—$64 less than projected. By the end of March, they'd saved a total of $455 (the $91 projected monthly savings for three months plus $182 extra), and they felt more comfortable about managing their finances than ever before. Arthur commented, "Mary and I have happily discovered that there are a lot of things to talk about besides money."

SAMPLE WORKSHEET 6:

Are the Burnses Staying on Course?

	Jan.	Feb.	Mar.	Apr.	May	Jun.
(L1) Total Monthly Income (from Worksheet 4)	1475	1448	1485			
(L2) Total Monthly Expenses (from Worksheet 5)	1188	1421	1344			
(L3) Total Monthly Savings or Deficit (L1 – L2)	287	27	41			
(L4) Projected Monthly Savings or Deficit (from Worksheet 3, L17, C5)	91	91	91			
(L5) Extra Savings or Deficit (L3 – L4)	196	-64	50			
(L6) Cumulative Total	196	132	182			

Selecting the Best Credit Card

Bank credit cards such as Visa and MasterCard have become popular because they make shopping simpler and eliminate the need to carry a lot of cash. But credit cards are so handy and easy to use that many people run up large debts without even realizing it. Then they're faced with the problem of having to pay them off. If you're carrying burdensome credit card debts from month to month and can't seem to whittle them down, avoid using your cards and start paying only cash for your purchases. Once your debt is down to zero and you've started to save money regularly, then decide whether you really need to use a credit card again. If you do, plan your charges so that you can pay off each month's balance in full. Choose your card carefully. Banks differ in the ways they figure your credit card balance, the interest rates they charge, and their annual fees. When shopping for a bank credit card, first ask the bank to send you an application. Then, after you've read the information, call the customer service department and ask the representative these questions to help you select the one that will cost the least.

1.   What is the annual percentage rate?   _____

The annual percentage rate (often abbreviated APR) is the interest rate charged on credit card purchases. The average is about 18% (1.5% monthly), but some lenders charge more than 20% and others as low as 11.5%. You can obtain a list of current credit card interest rates by sending $1 to: Bankcard Holders of America, 333 Pennsylvania Avenue SE, Washington, DC 20003.

2.   If I pay the previous month's balance in full on or before the payment due date shown on the bill, will I be charged any interest for the current month's purchases?   _____

About half of the credit card issuers will allow you a "free ride" on this month's purchases. This means that from the date that you purchase an item up until the date that payment is due, you don't owe a penny of interest. About 15% of the issuers will charge you daily interest from the date of every purchase, even if you paid the preceding month's balance in full. Avoid these!

3.   If I pay only part of the previous month's balance, what will I be charged?   _____

Most bank card issuers charge interest on the unpaid balance and all new purchases. However, about 20% of the issuers now charge "retroactive interest" if you don't pay the full amount of your bill by the due date. These banks will charge you interest from the date of purchase on all the previous month's purchases as well as interest from the date of purchase on this month's purchases. If you don't expect to pay each month's bill in full on or before the due date, avoid these, also.

4.   What is the annual fee?   _____

Annual fees range from nothing to $35 or more. A bank that charges no annual fee may be one that charges you interest from the date of purchase. This is likely to wind up being more costly for you than a bank card that charges you $35 a year and allows you a free ride on each month's purchases. Similarly, bank cards that charge a low rate of interest may make it up by charging from the date of purchase. If you pay each month's bill in full and avoid cards that charge from the date of purchase, you won't owe any interest, so it doesn't matter what rate they charge.

When you've decided which charge card, or cards, is the right one for your financial situation, transfer the account number to the credit card inventory on Worksheet 14, on page 108.

Where Do You Want To Go?

OBJECTIVE: To plan for your financial security. How much can you expect your savings to grow? If you're unable to save, or if you're spending capital, how long will your money last?

WHAT YOU WILL NEED

Completed Worksheets 1 and 2

Now that you've taken control of your financial situation, where are you going? If you're able to save some of what you earn each month, how much will your savings be worth five or ten years from now? If you're dipping into capital, when will you run out of money? Your primary financial goal is to maintain your lifestyle and to avoid becoming dependent upon others for financial support.

Are You Able to Save Part of Your Income?

If you determined in Worksheet 3 that you are saving part of your income, then your net worth will continue to grow from your savings and the power of compounding. Compounding means reinvestment of earnings. For example, if you deposit money in an interest-bearing account at your bank, the interest earned during the current month is added to your account so that next month you earn interest on your new higher balance. If you allow your account to continue to compound in this manner, eventually it will double in value. You can calculate how long this will take with a simple formula called the rule of 72: divide the annual interest rate you expect to earn into the number 72 and the resulting figure is the number of years it will take for your money to double. For example, if you deposit $1,000 in an account that compounds interest annually at 8%, divide 8 into 72 and the result —9—is the number of years it will take for your account to be worth $2,000. Since most accounts compound more frequently than annually (many compound your interest daily), it's likely that your account will double in even less than nine years. In effect, a dollar saved is really more than a dollar earned because that dollar can be put to work to earn interest for you. On the other hand, a dollar spent is more than a dollar lost because you've given up its earnings potential.

Even if your living expenses consume all that you earn, the portion of your net worth that's in a savings account or invested in growth assets such as stocks or real estate (your home) is likely to compound in value over time.

It's valuable to know how much you'll be worth at some future date because someday you may need or want to draw on your savings and assets. If you have not yet retired or if you are working part time, one day that source of income will cease. The death of a spouse will also result in lower earnings because Social Security benefits will be lower and pension benefits may decline or cease.

Do You Need to Dip Into Capital?

If you are unable to maintain your lifestyle on your present income, you'll have to either change your lifestyle or dip into your accumulated capital in order to maintain your independence. There's nothing wrong with depleting your net worth as long as your money outlasts you. If you've made sacrifices during your younger years in order to accumulate your nest egg and you want to enjoy it now, remember the bumper sticker "I'm Spending My Children's Inheritance." Go ahead and do it!

Making certain that your money outlasts you means getting in touch with your own mortality. You have to make an assumption about how long you (and your spouse) can expect to live and then calculate how much you can spend each year so that you won't run out of money. Because heredity plays a significant role in determining your life expectancy, you can obtain a reasonable estimate by averaging your parents' ages when they died (if your parents died from accidental causes, use an average of your grandparents', aunts' or uncles', or siblings' ages instead). If you're a 65-year-old woman and your parents lived to their mid-80s (or if they're still living), you can expect to live another twenty years or so. Tack on an extra five years or more if you're in good health or want to ensure a legacy for your children.

When Should You Retire?

The road you take is based on many factors, including your health, your satisfaction with your job, your relationship with your spouse, and how you plan to spend your time after you stop working. Often, these factors are at odds with one another. For example, if you're in good health, you may have the desire to continue working and yet also want more time for leisure activities. Or, you may want to retire early—say at age 62—but recognize that you'll have to make do on a smaller income for the rest of your life. Because both monetary and personal considerations can conflict, there are no simple answers that will work for everyone. You must choose which path makes the most sense, based on your unique, individual situation. If this were a purely economic decision, it could be simply stated: the longer you expect to live, the longer you should postpone retirement. The earlier you retire, the lower your income from pensions, Social Security, and investments.

No matter what your age is today, you can obtain a written estimate of your future Social Security monthly retirement benefits, disability benefits, and survivor benefits by filing form SSA-7004, which requests the age you plan to retire (62, 65, or 70) and an estimate of your expected annual earnings from now until retirement. To get form SSA-7004, call 800-937-2000 or write the Consumer Information Center, Dept. 55, Social Security Administration, Pueblo, CO 81009.

If you're employed by a large company, the personnel department or benefits counselor can explain your retirement options. Many companies also sponsor pre-retirement seminars, which are designed to educate you and help you plan for the future. The following is a summary of the pros and cons of your retirement options.

Early Retirement (Age 62 or Earlier)

PROS

1.   You can begin receiving Social Security benefits three years earlier than standard retirement, at age 62. The monthly benefit will be reduced by 20% of the amount you'd receive at age 65 (0.55% for each month prior to age 65).

2.   If your employer is cutting back on the work force, you may be offered attractive incentives to retire early.

3.   You'll have more leisure time to devote to sports, hobbies, travel, volunteer work, etc.

CONS

1. The reduced Social Security retirement benefit is permanent and will remain fixed (with the exception of cost-of-living increases) unless you go back to work. If you live beyond age 74, you'll receive fewer cumulative benefits than if you'd postponed retirement until 65.

2. Because Social Security retirement benefits are computed on the basis of work years prior to retirement, your non-earning years prior to age 62 will reduce your monthly benefit.

3. If you have any health problems, you may not be able to obtain health insurance and you and your spouse won't be covered by Medicare until you're 65. Even if you're in good health, it's likely that insurance protection will be very costly. (If you're laid off from work, however, you're entitled to enroll in your former employer's group plan for at least eighteen months, as mandated by the Consolidated Omnibus Budget Reconciliation Act of 1985.)

4. Because of lower earnings, you may not be able to avail yourself of more costly retirement activities, such as travel and hobbies. You may have to give up some of the things you could afford when you were working.

Late Retirement (After Age 65)

PROS

1. If you enjoy working, you're likely to stay healthier longer. Many seniors who like their work find it difficult to adjust to a non-scheduled lifestyle. The activities they enjoyed as hobbies or diversions while they were working full time aren't suitable as work replacements. When you work all week, you may look forward to fishing on weekends, but it may not be as much fun when it's the only thing you do.

2. If you postpone receipt of Social Security benefits beyond age 65, you'll receive a larger monthly payment when benefits start. Each year you work beyond age 65 entitles you to an additional 3% in benefits, up to a maximum of 15% at age 70. Starting for people who reach 65 in 1990 and later, the additional annual benefit will be increased gradually until it reaches 8% in 2009. In addition, your benefit may be larger if it's based on a higher earnings history. After age 70, you're entitled to work full time and still receive the full amount of your Social Security benefit.

3.   Your company pension is likely to be greater.

CONS

1.   You won't have as much time available for leisure activities.

Part-Time Employment

PROS

1.   Beginning at age 62, you can earn up to a certain amount (a ceiling that's set each year) and still receive Social Security benefits. Every $2 in earnings above that amount reduces your benefit by $1 (this will be improved to $3 for every $1 after 1990).

2.   The income you receive augments Social Security, pension, and investment income and can provide you with a better lifestyle.

3.   You can continue to keep busy and active and have more time for leisure activities than if you worked full time.

CONS

1.   It may be difficult to find satisfying part-time work.

2.   Part-time jobs usually pay less (on an hourly basis) than full-time and offer no employee benefits.

Your Spouse's Benefit

It's possible to earn a benefit of your own and also qualify for 50% of your spouse's benefit, but you can't earn two full benefits. Usually, you're paid the higher amount. For example, if you're entitled to $150 on your own earnings and $200 on your spouse's earnings (½ of your spouse's $400 benefit), you'll get $200. If you retire early and your spouse continues to work, when your spouse retires, you'll get an increase based on your spouse's benefit. If your spouse later goes back to work, you'll continue to receive your own benefit, but it will be reduced. For example, if your own benefit—say, $150—is reduced by $30 because of early retirement and you later become eligible for a benefit of $200 because your spouse returns to work, you'll be paid $170 ($200 − $30). If your spouse dies, you will be paid the full widow's or widower's benefit, even if you were receiving a reduced benefit. If you survive two spouses, your benefit will be based on the higher record.

Worksheet 7: Calculating Optimal Retirement Benefits

Complete Worksheet 7, using the compounding tables on pages 53–54. Table 1, "Compounding a Single Sum of $1," determines the value of your spendable net worth at some future date. Your spendable net worth is the portion of your net worth that's comprised of income-producing and growth assets that could be converted to cash, if necessary. It excludes the value of your personal assets, which tend to decline in value and can be sold for only a fraction of what you paid.

To calculate the value of your spendable net worth on the date you retire or begin withdrawing capital, use Table 1 to locate the intersection of the number of years to retirement and the current money market rate, which you can obtain by calling your bank or savings and loan. Money market rates in the past have kept pace with inflation, so if prices go up, so should the return on your capital. Assuming you plan to retire in five years, and the money market rate is currently 6%, the intersection of these two figures—called the compounding factor—is 1.338. Multiply this factor by the value of your present spendable net worth to determine what your spendable net worth will be at retirement. Assuming your spendable net worth is now $150,000, you can expect it to be $200,700 ($150,000 × 1.338) in five years if it's invested or grows at an annual rate of 6%.

Table 2, "Compounding a Regular Annual Savings of $1," uses the same method to determine how much your annual savings will be worth at retirement or other future date. For example, if you're able to raise $3,000 each year and expect an annual earnings growth rate of 6%, you can expect your savings to be worth $16,911 ($3,000 × 5.637) in five years. Your total spendable net worth in five years will equal the sum of your compounded spendable net worth ($200,700) and your compounded annual savings ($16,911), or $217,611.

If you are unable to live on your present income or plan to retire in the foreseeable future and begin drawing on your savings, complete Worksheet 8 to find out how much you can afford to spend each month so that your money will outlast you. The table at the bottom of this worksheet calculates the percentage of your spendable net worth that can be withdrawn each month so that your money will last the time period you choose. Like a compounding table, it factors in the continued growth of your assets during the withdrawal period (it assumes your money isn't tucked under a mattress, earning nothing). The rate you choose is the current money market rate, which you can obtain by calling your bank or savings and loan.

Table 1: *Compounding a Single Sum of $1*

Period	1%	2%	4%	6%	7%	8%	9%	10%	11%	12%	14%	16%	20%
1	1.010	1.020	1.040	1.060	1.070	1.080	1.090	1.100	1.110	1.120	1.139	1.160	1.200
2	1.020	1.040	1.082	1.124	1.145	1.166	1.188	1.210	1.232	1.254	1.297	1.346	1.440
3	1.030	1.061	1.125	1.191	1.225	1.260	1.295	1.331	1.368	1.405	1.478	1.561	1.728
4	1.041	1.082	1.170	1.262	1.311	1.360	1.412	1.464	1.518	1.574	1.683	1.811	2.074
5	1.051	1.104	1.217	1.338	1.403	1.469	1.539	1.611	1.685	1.762	1.917	2.100	2.488
6	1.062	1.126	1.265	1.419	1.501	1.587	1.677	1.772	1.870	1.974	2.183	2.436	2.986
7	1.072	1.149	1.316	1.504	1.606	1.714	1.828	1.949	2.076	2.211	2.487	2.826	3.583
8	1.083	1.172	1.369	1.594	1.718	1.851	1.993	2.144	2.305	2.476	2.833	3.278	4.300
9	1.094	1.195	1.423	1.689	1.838	1.999	2.172	2.358	2.558	2.773	3.226	3.803	5.160
10	1.105	1.219	1.480	1.791	1.967	2.159	2.367	2.594	2.839	3.106	3.675	4.411	6.192
11	1.116	1.243	1.539	1.898	2.105	2.332	2.580	2.853	3.152	3.479	4.186	5.117	7.430
12	1.127	1.268	1.601	2.012	2.252	2.518	2.813	3.138	3.498	3.896	4.767	5.936	8.916
13	1.138	1.294	1.665	2.133	2.410	2.720	3.066	3.452	3.883	4.363	5.430	6.886	10.699
14	1.149	1.319	1.732	2.261	2.579	2.937	3.342	3.797	4.310	4.887	6.185	7.988	12.839
15	1.161	1.346	1.801	2.397	2.759	3.172	3.642	4.177	4.785	5.474	7.045	9.266	15.407
16	1.173	1.373	1.873	2.540	2.952	3.426	3.970	4.595	5.311	6.130	8.024	10.748	18.488
17	1.184	1.400	1.948	2.693	3.159	3.700	4.328	5.054	5.895	6.866	9.139	12.468	22.186
18	1.196	1.428	2.026	2.854	3.380	3.996	4.717	5.560	6.544	7.690	10.409	14.463	26.623
19	1.208	1.457	2.107	3.026	3.617	4.316	5.142	6.116	7.263	8.613	11.856	16.777	31.948
20	1.220	1.486	2.191	3.207	3.870	4.661	5.604	6.727	8.062	9.646	13.504	19.461	38.338
25	1.282	1.641	2.666	4.292	5.427	6.848	8.623	10.835	13.585	17.000	25.888	40.874	95.396
30	1.348	1.811	3.243	5.743	7.612	10.063	13.268	17.449	22.892	29.960	49.626	85.850	237.376

Table 2: *Compounding a Regular Annual Savings of $1*

Period	1%	2%	4%	6%	7%	8%	9%	10%	11%	12%	14%	16%	20%
1	1.000	1.000	1.000	1.000	1.000	1.000	1.000	1.000	1.000	1.000	1.000	1.000	1.000
2	2.010	2.020	2.040	2.060	2.070	2.080	2.090	2.100	2.110	2.120	2.139	2.160	2.200
3	3.030	3.060	3.122	3.184	3.215	3.246	3.278	3.310	3.342	3.374	3.436	3.506	3.640
4	4.060	4.122	4.246	4.375	4.440	4.506	4.573	4.641	4.710	4.779	4.914	5.066	5.368
5	5.101	5.204	5.416	5.637	5.751	5.867	5.985	6.105	6.228	6.353	6.597	6.877	7.442
6	6.152	6.308	6.633	6.975	7.153	7.336	7.523	7.716	7.913	8.115	8.514	8.977	9.930
7	7.214	7.434	7.898	8.394	8.654	8.923	9.200	9.487	9.783	10.089	10.697	11.414	12.916
8	8.286	8.583	9.214	9.897	10.260	10.637	11.028	11.436	11.859	12.300	13.184	14.240	16.499
9	9.369	9.755	10.583	11.491	11.978	12.488	13.021	13.579	14.164	14.776	16.017	17.519	20.799
10	10.462	10.950	12.006	13.181	13.816	14.487	15.193	15.937	16.722	17.549	19.243	21.321	25.959
11	11.567	12.169	13.486	14.972	15.784	16.645	17.560	18.531	19.561	20.655	22.918	25.733	32.150
12	12.683	13.412	15.026	16.870	17.888	18.977	20.141	21.384	22.713	24.133	27.104	30.850	39.581
13	13.809	14.680	16.627	18.882	20.141	21.495	22.953	24.523	26.212	28.029	31.871	36.786	48.497
14	14.947	15.974	18.292	21.015	22.550	24.215	26.019	27.975	30.095	32.393	37.301	43.672	59.196
15	16.097	17.293	20.024	23.276	25.129	27.152	29.361	31.772	34.405	37.280	43.486	51.660	72.035
16	17.258	18.639	21.825	25.673	27.888	30.324	33.003	35.950	39.190	42.753	50.531	60.925	87.442
17	18.430	20.012	23.698	28.213	30.840	33.750	36.974	40.545	44.501	48.884	58.555	71.673	105.931
18	19.615	21.412	25.645	30.906	33.999	37.450	41.301	45.599	50.396	55.750	67.694	84.141	128.117
19	20.811	22.841	27.671	33.760	37.379	41.446	46.018	51.159	56.939	63.440	78.103	98.603	154.740
20	22.019	24.297	29.778	36.786	40.995	45.762	51.160	57.275	64.203	72.052	89.960	115.380	186.688
25	28.243	32.030	41.646	54.865	63.249	73.106	84.701	98.347	114.413	133.334	179.048	249.214	471.981
30	34.785	40.568	56.085	79.058	94.461	113.283	136.308	164.494	199.021	241.333	349.829	530.312	1181.882

WORKSHEET 7

How Much Will Your Money Grow?

(L1) What is your present net worth?
(from Worksheet 1, L10) _____

(L2) What is the value of your personal assets?
(from Worksheet 1, L4) _____

(L3) What is your spendable net worth?
(subtract L2 from L1) _____

(L4) What is the current money market rate?
(obtain figure from your bank or financial section of newspaper) _____

(L5) In how many years will you retire (or begin withdrawing capital)? _____

(L6) What is your compounding factor for L5 years?
(on Table 1 locate the intersection of the percentage shown on L4
with the number of years indicated on L5) _____

(L7) What will your spendable net worth be in L5 years?
(multiply L3 by L6) _____

(L8) What are your monthly savings? (if 0, enter 0 on L11 and go to L12)
(from Worksheet 3, L17, C5) _____

(L9) What are your annual savings?
(multiply L8 by 12) _____

(L10) What is your annual savings factor for L5 years?
(on Table 2 locate the intersection of the percentage shown on L4 with the
number of years indicated on L5) _____

(L11) What will your annual savings be worth in L5 years?
(multiply L9 by L10) _____

(L12) What is your total projected spendable net worth in L5 years?
(L7 + L11) _____

WORKSHEET 8

How Much Can You Afford to Spend Each Month?

(L1) Until what age do you expect to live? _____
      (add five to average of parents' ages at death)

(L2) How many years must your capital last? _____
      (if you're now withdrawing capital, subtract your present age from L1)
      (if you expect to begin withdrawing capital in the future, subtract your age at
      withdrawal from L1)

(L3) What is (or will be) your spendable net worth? _____
      (if you're now withdrawing capital, use figure from Worksheet 7, L3)
      (if you expect to begin withdrawing capital in the future, use figure from
      Worksheet 7, L12)

(L4) What is the current money market rate? _____
      (obtain figure from your bank or financial section of newspaper)

(L5) What percentage of your spendable net worth can you spend (will you be able to _____
      spend) each month?
      (using table below, find intersection of values listed for L1 and L4 above)

(L6) How much can you afford to spend (will you be able to afford to spend) each _____
      month? (L3 × L5 × .01)

Current Money Market Rate	Number of Years Money Must Last													
	2	4	6	8	10	12	14	16	18	20	25	30	35	40
5%	4.39	2.31	1.62	1.27	1.07	0.93	0.83	0.76	0.71	0.66	0.59	0.54	0.51	0.49
7%	4.48	2.40	1.71	1.37	1.07	1.03	0.94	0.87	0.82	0.78	0.71	0.67	0.64	0.63
9%	4.57	2.49	1.81	1.47	1.27	1.14	1.05	0.99	0.94	0.90	0.84	0.81	0.79	0.78
11%	4.67	2.59	1.91	1.58	1.38	1.26	1.17	1.11	1.07	1.04	0.99	0.96	0.94	0.93
13%	4.76	2.69	2.01	1.69	1.50	1.38	1.30	1.24	1.21	1.18	1.13	1.11	1.10	1.09

> ### Sample: The Burnses Calculate Their Retirement Options

Arthur's parents lived to their early 70s, so he expects to live another ten years (he's now 68). Mary's mother died in an accident, but her father and two aunts lived to their late 80s, so she calculates that she'll live another twenty-four years (she's 64). Arthur's concerned with how much money Mary will have to live on if he predeceases her and his company pension benefits stop. Using Worksheet 7, they calculate the compounded growth of their spendable net worth and savings during the next ten years, at which time Arthur's pension may cease.

First they calculate the growth in value of their spendable net worth (net worth exclusive of personal assets). This is the portion of their net worth that includes their home equity, savings accounts, and investments—assets that are likely to increase in value and could be converted to cash if funds were needed. If this amount ($90,700) were compounded at the current money market rate (7%), it would be worth $178,407 (L7) in ten years. Assuming their $91/month projected

SAMPLE WORKSHEET 7:

How Much Will the Burnses' Money Grow?

(L1) What is your present net worth? (from Worksheet 1, L10) — *103,200*

(L2) What is the value of your personal assets? (from Worksheet 1, L4) — *12,500*

(L3) What is your spendable net worth? (subtract L2 from L1) — *90,700*

(L4) What is the current money market rate? (obtain figure from your bank or financial section of newspaper) — *7%*

(L5) In how many years will you retire (or begin withdrawing capital)? — *10*

(L6) What is your compounding factor for L5 years? (on Table 1 locate the intersection of the percentage shown on L4 with the number of years indicated on L5) — *1.967*

(L7) What will your spendable net worth be in L5 years? (multiply L3 by L6) — *178,407*

(L8) What are your monthly savings? (if 0, enter 0 on L11 and go to L12) (from Worksheet 3, L17, C5) — *91*

(L9) What are your annual savings? (multiply L8 by 12) — *1,092*

(L10) What is your annual savings factor for L5 years? (on Table 2 locate the intersection of the percentage shown on L4 with the number of years indicated on L5) — *13.816*

(L11) What will your annual savings be worth in L5 years? (multiply L9 by L10) — *15,087*

(L12) What is your total projected spendable net worth in L5 years? (L7 + L11) — *193,494*

monthly savings compounded at the same rate, their total projected net worth in ten years (compounded savings plus growth in net worth) would be $193,494 (L12).

The Burnses were then able to calculate how much money Mary could spend each month if Arthur predeceased her by fourteen years and his pension plan benefits stopped, by using Worksheet 8.

The amount Mary will be able to spend will depend on the rate of growth or compounding (7%) and the number of years the money must last (fourteen). According to the table, Mary can withdraw 0.94% of her spendable net worth ($193,493) each month—or $1,819. She said, "We were raised with the philosophy that it's a sin to dip into capital, but that was true in the days when people didn't live as long. Our children are grown and self-sufficient, so they don't need our money. We might as well enjoy it ourselves." Arthur added a word of caution: "We're not kidding ourselves by ignoring the fact that health care costs or other unforeseen problems could eat up our nest egg, so we don't plan to spend as much as the worksheet indicates. But neither are we going to worry about dipping into our savings."

SAMPLE WORKSHEET 8:

How Much Can Mary Burns Afford to Spend Each Month?

(L1) Until what age do you expect to live? _88_
(add five to average of parents' ages at death)

(L2) How many years must your capital last? _14_
(if you're now withdrawing capital, subtract your present age from L1)
(if you expect to begin withdrawing capital in the future, subtract your age at withdrawal from L1)

(L3) What is (or will be) your spendable net worth? _193,494_
(if you're now withdrawing capital, use figure from Worksheet 7, L3)
(if you expect to begin withdrawing capital in the future, use figure from Worksheet 7, L12)

(L4) What is the current money market rate? _7%_
(obtain figure from your bank or financial section of newspaper)

(L5) What percentage of your spendable net worth can you spend (will you be able to spend) each month? _.94_
(using table below, find intersection of values listed for L1 and L4 above)

(L6) How much can you afford to spend (will you be able to afford to spend) each month? (L3 × L5 × .01) _1,819_

Current Money Market Rate	Number of Years Money Must Last													
	2	4	6	8	10	12	14	16	18	20	25	30	35	40
5%	4.39	2.31	1.62	1.27	1.07	0.93	0.83	0.76	0.71	0.66	0.59	0.54	0.51	0.49
7%	4.48	2.40	1.71	1.37	1.07	1.03	0.94	0.87	0.82	0.78	0.71	0.67	0.64	0.63
9%	4.57	2.49	1.81	1.47	1.27	1.14	1.05	0.99	0.94	0.90	0.84	0.81	0.79	0.78
11%	4.67	2.59	1.91	1.58	1.38	1.26	1.17	1.11	1.07	1.04	0.99	0.96	0.94	0.93
13%	4.76	2.69	2.01	1.69	1.50	1.38	1.30	1.24	1.21	1.18	1.13	1.11	1.10	1.09

<table>
<tr><td>

Countdown to Retirement

</td><td>

If you expect to retire in three years or less, you should start planning now. Circle the following dates on your calendar and check off each step as it's completed.

</td></tr>
</table>

Six Months Before Retirement

1.   From your local Social Security office, obtain copies of:

"Thinking About Retiring?" (SSA Publication #05-10055)
"Your Social Security" (SSA Publication #05-10035)
"How Work Affects Your Social Security Checks" (SSA Publication #05-10069)
"Estimating Your Social Security Retirement Check" (SSA Publication #05-10070)

2.   From your local Social Security office, obtain a copy of Form SSA-700, "Request for Statement of Earnings." Complete it, specifically requesting a monthly benefit estimate. After receiving the form, the Social Security Administration will provide you with a computer print-out of your earnings up to the year prior to the last calendar year and your estimated benefits at age 65. There is no charge for this service.

3.   If you'll be 65 in six months, obtain copies from your local Social Security office of:

"What You Should Know About Medicare" (SSA Publication #05-10043)
"Guide to Health Insurance for People with Medicare" (Publication #HCFA 02110)

4.   If you're covered by a company pension plan, schedule an appointment with your company's benefits counselor to discuss retirement options and continuation of health care insurance.

Three Months Before Retirement

Visit your local Social Security office to:

● apply for Social Security benefits.
● if you're 65, enroll in Medicare.

Two Months Before Retirement

1. Decide how to take distribution of company pension plan.
2. Gather information on private health insurance to augment Medicare.

One Month Before Retirement

Make a decision on a private health insurance carrier.

It would be nice if you could calculate exactly how much money you will need for your goals and not have to worry any more. But such is not the case. Life, as you already know, is a journey fraught with many obstacles—health problems, inflation, unforeseen expenses, uncertain interest rates. Starting out on the right road doesn't guarantee you'll get where you're going, but recognizing obstacles and taking the necessary detours will. In the next chapters, you'll learn how to prepare for and overcome these obstacles.

HOW SHOULD YOU WITHDRAW YOUR RETIREMENT PLAN?

If you're entitled to receive benefits from your company's pension plan, schedule an appointment with your benefits counselor to find out how much you can expect to receive and what withdrawal options are available. Discuss the following:

1. Many companies will allow you to withdraw your benefit as a lump sum, to invest as you choose. Others require that you take your benefit as a monthly income (annuity). The amount you receive depends not only upon your employment earnings but also on your decision whether to provide spouse's benefits if your spouse outlives you.

What pension plan withdrawal options are available? _____

2. If you have the choice of a monthly income (annuity) or a lump sum withdrawal, your decision rests on whether you could do as well investing the money as the monthly return your company provides. Because lump sum distributions cause a drain on a company's retirement plan assets, employers can use a formula for calculating lump sum benefits that

makes this choice less attractive to retiring employees. Divide the annual annuity income you'd receive by the amount you'd receive as a lump sum to determine your percentage return on your pension. If it's the same or less than you could expect to earn on the money yourself, you're better off with the lump sum withdrawal. For example, if your choice is between a monthly income of $500 or a lump sum benefit of $60,000, your annual income of $6,000 represents a 10% return on your pension. If you could invest your money at that rate you'd come out ahead with the lump sum because you'd earn the same monthly income as with the annuity option and the $60,000 would remain intact. You could draw on it if you needed additional funds or leave it to your heirs. The annuity terminates when you (or your spouse, if a joint annuity) die.

What will the monthly income be?　　　　　　＿＿＿＿＿＿＿＿＿
The lump sum?　　　　　　　　　　　　　　＿＿＿＿＿＿＿＿＿

3.　If you withdraw your benefit as a lump sum, you can choose between rolling it over into an Individual Retirement Account (IRA) within sixty days and deferring taxes, or paying the taxes in the year of the distribution. If you are 50 years of age on or before January 1, 1986, lump sum distributions are taxed as though the money is received over a period of ten years rather than all at once. Generally speaking, if you plan to postpone withdrawal of funds from the IRA for more than five years, you're better off with a rollover.

What will be the tax impact of a lump sum
distribution?　　　　　　　　　　　　　　＿＿＿＿＿＿＿＿＿

4.　If you contributed part of your earnings to the plan, your benefits will be non-taxable to the extent of your contribution percentage (since these earnings were already taxed). If you choose the annuity, part of your monthly benefit will be a tax-free return of capital; if you choose the lump sum withdrawal, part of the distribution will not be subject to tax.

What percentage of the monthly benefit will be
tax-free?　　　　　　　　　　　　　　　　＿＿＿＿＿＿＿＿＿

What percentage of the lump sum will be tax-free?＿＿＿＿＿＿＿＿＿

5.　The contingent annuitant option assures continuance of income to a surviving spouse or other relative upon your death. You can choose to have the survivor receive the same monthly benefit for the rest of his or her life, half the monthly benefit, or any other percentage. Naturally, your decision will determine the amount of the monthly benefit you receive— the greater the amount of the survivor's percentage, the lower your monthly benefit. For example, if you were to select the straight annuity option, under which monthly payments terminate at your death, you could receive as much as 33% more each month than if you chose the joint-and-survivor option, which pays the same monthly benefit for the lives of you and your spouse. Your spouse must provide written consent to any option other than the joint-and-survivor annuity.

How much will a straight annuity pay?   _____
A joint-and-survivor?   _____

If You Can't Make It— Other Sources of Financial Security

OBJECTIVE: To locate other sources of income. If you own your home, can you free up the equity? Should you sell your home and rent, instead? Are there other living arrangements you should investigate? Should you apply for government benefits? How can you pay off your bills and get started on the right track?

WHAT YOU WILL NEED
> Home mortgage amortization schedule
> Costs of home improvements and additions

If you're unable to make ends meet, due to medical costs, loss of income, or increased expenses, it's likely that you can either reduce expenses further or draw on assets or other sources of income, some of which you may not have considered before. Now is the time to take a look at these.

Turning Your Home Equity Into Income: Home Equity Conversion

One excellent source of income is the equity in your home. If you've owned your home for several years, your equity (the current market value less the outstanding mortgage balance) has increased steadily as a result of two factors. The first is inflation—a general rise in real estate prices that's boosted property values all over the country. If you bought your home fifteen years ago, it's likely that today it's worth twice or three times what you paid. The second factor is mortgage paydown. Every mortgage payment you make consists of part interest and part principal; your principal payment increases your net worth in the same way as a deposit in your bank account. The difference is, you can easily withdraw the interest or principal from your bank account, while your home equity is locked up until you sell your home.

Because many older Americans have a large portion of their net worth tied up in homes with low or no mortgages and they need funds in order to pay medical bills or other expenses, new government and private programs have been developed which can turn your home into a source of income. Each of the following four plans is designed to help you tap part or all of the equity in your home.

1. Would you be willing to sell your home if you knew you could continue to live in it for as long as you wished and receive a monthly income from it, too?

A *sale leaseback* arranges for the sale of your home to a family member or investor and guarantees you a lifetime lease. You can arrange to receive the sale proceeds as a lump sum payment, monthly income, or some of both. The person who purchases your home becomes responsible for taxes, maintenance, and property upkeep, while you continue to live in it for life. This plan matches older homeowners in need of cash with investors in need of tax benefits.

2. Are you unwilling to sell your home but want it to produce income for you?

A *reverse mortgage (RM)* arranges monthly loan advances for a set number of years (called a fixed-term RM) or for as long as you live in your home (called an open-ended RM). Because of the cost to the lender and the potential risk that the home may decline in value, the loan amount is usually between 60% and 80% of the appraised value. A fixed-term RM loan must be repaid in full at the end of the term, which will usually require sale of the home. An open-ended RM, on the other hand, is repaid when the home is sold or the owner dies. Generally, the interest charged is compounded, creating a situation in which the total accumulated interest may exceed the amount of cash received by the homeowner. If the home has appreciated, the owner may be able to renegotiate the loan.

The *line-of-credit reverse mortgage*, which permits homeowners to choose when and in what amounts they can make loan advances, is designed for coping with sporadic or unexpected expenses. The Maryland and Virginia state housing finance authorities are the first to sponsor this arrangement, beginning in 1988.

Your personal residence is not included in the determination of whether your financial condition qualifies you for government Medicaid benefits that pay for long-term nursing-home care. You and/or your spouse can receive Medicaid benefits and still hold title to a valuable asset that is likely to increase in value. If you choose the reverse mortgage, you may be able to generate additional monthly income and still qualify for Medicaid benefits.

3. Would you like to borrow money in order to repair or renovate your home and postpone repayment indefinitely?

A *deferred payment loan* allows you to take out a low- or no-interest loan and defer repayment until the property is sold or transferred. The loan is repaid out of sale proceeds or, if the owner dies, out of the estate settlement.

4. Would you like to postpone payment of property taxes indefinitely?

A *property tax deferral* is a lien against your property for the annual property tax liability plus interest (usually lower than market rates). Like the deferred payment loan, above, it's eventually repaid out of sale proceeds or, if the owner dies, out of estate settlement.

Because home equity conversion is a major (and sometimes irreversible) financial decision, and all four plans involve complex legal documents, it's advisable to seek the advice of a knowledgeable attorney who can help you assess the strengths and weaknesses of the plans offered in your community. Most areas where programs are available also offer impartial third-party counseling to assist homeowners in evaluating the appropriateness of this option for them.

Home Equity Loans

Home equity conversion is often confused with home equity loans, but these are quite different arrangements. A home equity loan is a second mortgage on your property. It's available through major banks and brokerage firms in many states, and it enables individuals to borrow money for a period of up to fifteen years, using their home as collateral. The lending institution extends a line of credit of up to 80% of your equity, which you may withdraw in a lump sum or as you need it. Origination fees can run as high as 2% of the credit line, and there may be other costs, including appraisal and title search charges, survey fees, and mortgage taxes. Your interest rate is pegged to the prime rate (generally 2% to

4% higher), which means that if interest rates rise, you'll owe more. In addition, the lender may require that you pay back interest and principal regularly or may call in the loan after a certain time period. If you're not able to come up with the money, your home may be repossessed. Home equity loans have become popular because the interest you pay is fully tax-deductible, while other consumer loan interest payments are only partially deductible. They are not suitable for most elderly individuals, whose need for capital is ongoing and who may not be able to pay back the loan.

Alternate Living Arrangements

Many older people make changes in their living arrangements in response to a crisis. If you take the time to examine the alternatives before a crisis occurs, your choice is likely to be a happier one for everyone concerned. There are many housing choices available for seniors. The type you select depends on these factors: your financial situation; whether you have your own home or have family members or friends you want to live with or near; the status of your health; your need for independence and privacy; your requirements for assistance with meal preparation, personal care, and housekeeping; your desire for companionship and stimulating activities; and your need for transportation.

Should You Consider a Shared Living Arrangement?

1. Are you in good health but unable to afford the expenses of having your own apartment or home? YES NO

Consider an arrangement in which you offer your services as a caretaker, housesitter, or companion to someone who's willing to share their home. If you enjoy gardening, babysitting, or meal preparation, you may be able to work out an arrangement in which you exchange your services for a place to live. Some cities have house-matching programs that will help you find a suitable arrangement, or you could place an ad in your local newspaper or on your community center bulletin board.

2. Do you have your own home or apartment but desire help with household responsibilities or expenses? YES NO

If zoning permits, a home-sharing arrangement may be right for you, too. The agreement you make should be spelled out in a legal contract and may entail a monthly rent, an exchange of services (the boarder does the shopping, cooking, and cleaning in exchange for a place to live), or a combination of both. If you prefer to maintain separate quarters and your house is large enough, you could arrange to partition off part of it and create a separate apartment to be rented out.

3. Do you want to live with family but maintain your privacy?　　　　　　　　　　　　　　　　　　YES　　NO

An Elder Cottage Housing Opportunity (ECHO) may suit your needs. ECHO homes are small (one or two bedroom), relatively inexpensive (less than $20,000), portable units that can be placed in back of or alongside a home. Because they're detached from the main residence, both you and your family can maintain your privacy. Check with your local Area Agency on Aging and zoning department to find out if ECHO is available in your community.

4. Would you prefer not to be responsible for the day-to-day chores of cooking and cleaning?　　　　　　　　　　　　YES　　NO

A board-and-care home, which provides room, board, utilities, housekeeping, and laundry, may be an ideal arrangement. Staff members are on hand to make sure that all is well, and additional services, such as personal care, bathing, and social activities may also be provided. Before you consider such a facility, find out if the home complies with state licensing requirements. If you don't need all the services that are offered and want to reduce your costs, ask if you can pay for only those services you require, and make sure that all arrangements and fees are spelled out in a written contract. Board-and-care homes vary widely in their standards of service and cleanliness so it's important that you visit the home and talk with residents before you reach a decision.

5. Do you enjoy being with others on a regular basis?　　　　　　　　　　　　　　　　　　　　YES　　NO

A congregate housing facility, like a resort hotel, provides you with your own private quarters (including a kitchen), and meals are served in a central dining room. A professional staff of social workers, counselors, and nutritionists is on hand to administer services and direct social activities. Costs vary widely, depending on the facility and the services (transportation, housekeeping, shopping) you require. Before you sign a contract, make several visits to the facility and speak with both residents and staff members.

6. Do you want health and medical care to be readily available should you need it?　　　　　　　　　　　　　　　YES　　NO

Continuing care (also called life care) communities provide residents with individual living units, meals, and a wide variety of recreational activities along with the guarantee of 24-hour nursing care whenever necessary. Facilities range in size from 100 to 500 units and many have swimming pools and golf courses as well as organized classes and social activities. Generally, these are more costly than other housing arrangements. They often require a substantial entrance fee ($20,000 to $100,000) as well as a monthly fee ranging from $650 to $1,200 (with inflationary increases); this assures you of housing and services for the rest of your life, regardless of your health. Some offer full health care benefits, while others allow you to pay for care as needed. Find out if you can make an arrangement that suits your needs. Because of the large down payment, you want to be absolutely sure that you can count on the services that are promised. To find out about a facility you're considering, contact your state insurance, health, or social service office. Check also with the Better Business Bureau and speak with residents and their families and with local consumer groups. Before signing a contract, ask an attorney to review the agreement, the facility's statement of financial condition, and biographical information on the owners and sponsors. Be sure you understand the terms of the agreement. For instance, if you die or decide to leave, will a portion of your entrance fee be refunded? Under what conditions will fees be increased? Many states (including Arizona, California, Colorado, Florida, Illinois, Indiana, Maryland, Michigan, Minnesota, Missouri, Pennsylvania, and Virginia) have passed legislation regulating life care communities.

7. Do you require extensive or long-term health care?   YES   NO

Nursing homes provide 24-hour nursing care under a physician's supervision and only admit individuals who are referred by a doctor's order. If you do not require constant care but are unable to live alone, you'll receive intermediate care. You'll also receive skilled nursing care as needed for those conditions that don't require hospitalization. All state governments require that nursing homes be licensed, and state inspectors visit homes at least annually to determine their compliance with cleanliness and licensing requirements. Medicare, Medicaid, and medigap policies reimburse some, but not all, expenses. Determine your eligibility by contacting your state department of social services, welfare, or Social Security. "The Medicare Handbook" (Publication #HCFA-10050), available at your Social Security office, is another good source of information. Make certain that the services offered meet your needs, that the environment is clean and congenial, and that the visiting privileges suit you.

> *Obtaining Federal, State, and Local Benefits*

Have you looked into the possibility of receiving benefits from public or private organizations? While you are probably already receiving some benefits—Social Security and Medicare, for example—it's likely that there are many others you're unaware of. In the Washington, DC, area alone, over fifty programs and services benefit senior citizens.

Following are brief descriptions of government benefits to which you may be entitled. Phone or write for additional information. Also contact your local Area Agency on Aging or Information and Referral Office for information about state and local benefits, or if you're in the United Seniors Health Cooperative service area (Maryland, Virginia, Washington, DC), have an Eligibility Check-up.

SOCIAL SECURITY RETIREMENT BENEFITS

What Are They? Benefits are paid monthly upon retirement to workers who have contributed to the Social Security system for thirty-six quarters through payroll deductions, and to their surviving spouses and dependents. Retirement age is 65 unless the worker elects early retirement and receives reduced benefits, beginning at age 62.

Where to Apply: Call your local Social Security Administration office or Social Security Administration Regional Service Center.

SUPPLEMENTAL SECURITY INCOME BENEFITS

What Are They? Benefits are paid monthly to elderly, blind, or disabled people who have limited income and resources. To qualify in 1988, monthly income cannot exceed $374 ($552 for a married couple), and net worth (exclusive of home, car, personal belongings, and life insurance limited to $1,500 face value) cannot exceed $1,900 ($2,750 for a married couple). Ask your Social Security office to mail you the pamphlet "Guide to Supplemental Security Income" (SSA Publication #05-11015) if you think you may qualify. The maximum monthly benefit in 1988 is $354 ($532 for a married couple).

Where to Apply: Call your local Social Security Administration office or Social Security Administration Regional Service Center.

MEDICARE BENEFITS

What Are They? Medicare is a federally administered health insurance program for people 65 and older. It covers a portion of hospital and physicians' services.

Where to Apply: Call your local Social Security Administration office or Social Security Administration Regional Service Center and be sure to apply at least three months before your 65th birthday.

VETERANS' BENEFITS

What Are They? Veterans' benefits provide security to former armed services personnel, and to their families and survivors.

Where to Apply: Call or write your Veterans Administration Regional Office.

CIVIL SERVICE RETIREMENT BENEFITS

What Are They? The civil service program provides benefits to retired or disabled federal workers during their lifetime and to their survivors. To qualify, workers must have been continuously employed by the federal government or be civilian employees of the armed services for at least five years.

Where to Apply: Contact the personnel office of the agency for which you worked or: Office of Personnel Management Compensation Bureau, 1900 E Street NW, Washington, DC 20415. Telephone 202-632-7700.

CIVIL SERVICE SPOUSE BENEFITS

What Are They? The civil service program provides benefits to divorced or widowed spouses of federal employees. Benefits may be in the form of either a pension or a lump sum. Former spouses may also apply for health coverage under the Federal Employee Health Benefit Plan.

Where to Apply: Contact the personnel office of the agency for which you worked or: Office of Personnel Management Compensation Bureau, 1900 E Street NW, Washington, DC 20415. Telephone 202-632-7700.

CIVIL SERVICE LUMP-SUM BENEFITS

What Are They? All federal employees are entitled to a lump-sum benefit when they terminate employment, even if it is prior to retirement age.

Where to Apply: Contact the personnel office of the agency for which you worked or: Office of Personnel Management Compensation Bureau, 1900 E Street NW, Washington, DC 20415. Telephone 202-632-7700.

RAILROAD RETIREMENT BENEFITS

What Are They? Railroad retirement benefits provide a monthly cash payment to retired railroad workers and their spouses. Surviving spouses, minor children, and parents may also qualify. Employees with at least thirty years of service may retire with full benefits at age 60.

Where to Apply: Contact the nearest Railroad Retirement Board office or: The Railroad Retirement Board, 444 Pennsylvania Building, 425 13th Street NW, Washington, DC 20004. Telephone 202-724-0894.

FOREIGN SERVICE BENEFITS

What Are They? The Foreign Service provides retirement benefits to Foreign Service employees, spouses, and former spouses. Regulations for entitlement change frequently.

Where to Apply: Contact: U.S. Foreign Service, Retirement Division, Room 1251, Department of State, Washington, DC 20520. Telephone 202-632-3300.

HILL-BURTON HOSPITAL FUND BENEFITS

What Are They? In 1946, Congress passed a law that gave hospitals and other health care facilities funds for construction and modernization. In return, fund recipients must provide a certain percentage of services to persons unable to pay.

Where to Apply: Call the toll-free Hill-Burton Hotline: 800-638-0742.

MEDICAID BENEFITS

What Are They? Medicaid is a federal program, operated by the state, that helps needy individuals pay for medical care. Applicants must meet financial eligibility requirements.

Where to Apply: Contact the Department of Social Services in your area (look in your telephone directory under state listings).

FOOD STAMP BENEFITS

What Are They? Families with limited financial resources and low incomes may be entitled to food stamps, which can be used instead of cash for purchasing groceries.

Where to Apply: Contact the Department of Social Services in your area (look in your telephone directory under state listings).

UNEMPLOYMENT COMPENSATION BENEFITS

What Are They? Individuals who are able and willing to work but are unemployed through no fault of their own and who have been employed at least twenty weeks in the previous calendar year (eligibility requirements vary from state to state) may apply for benefits.

Where to Apply: Contact the Unemployment Compensation Division of your state Department of Labor and Employment Security (look in your telephone directory under state listings).

CIVILIAN HEALTH AND MEDICAL PROGRAM OF THE UNIFORMED
SERVICES (CHAMPUS) BENEFITS

What Are They: Individuals who are entitled to receive military
retired pay and their spouses and dependent children are eligible to
receive hospitalization, out-patient treatment and services, and prescription medication on a space-available basis. The government generally pays 75% of the cost. Benefits begin on the day your retired pay
becomes effective and end when you qualify for Medicare.

Where to Apply: Contact the Health Benefits Advisor (HBA) at
the nearest uniformed services medical facility.

Other Sources of Income

If you are unable to tap your home equity and
have exhausted sources of senior citizen benefits, there may be yet other ways to receive
additional income.

If you are physically able to work, many
localities provide employment opportunities that match the skills of
elderly workers with available part- or full-time jobs. Contact your
local or area Senior Community Service Employment Program office
to find out what's available in your community. More and more companies are eager to hire senior citizens because they've proven to be
experienced, reliable employees. If you are disabled or prefer to work
at home and have a marketable skill—carpentry or dressmaking, for
example—an advertisement in your local newspaper may keep you
quite busy. Craft fairs and flea markets are a way to generate income
from a hobby, such as doll- or quilt-making. Many older people have
discovered a latent artistic talent that they didn't have time to develop
in their younger, more active years. This can be the time to enjoy and
profit from it. A word of warning: don't be lured by "work at home"
mail solicitations or magazine advertisements that ask you to send
money. These companies prey on the poor and elderly and very few
are legitimate enterprises.

Do you have any paid-up life insurance contracts? You can convert
them into income producers by transferring their cash value to an
annuity that will pay you a monthly lifetime income—annuities are
discussed in Chapter Nine—or you can cash in the policies and pay off
debts or invest the proceeds yourself. If you have a company pension
plan, this may be another source of funds that you can either borrow
or withdraw.

You may also have valuable assets lying idle in your attic or cellar.
Your old books, magazines, phonograph records, and bric-a-brac could
be worth more than their original cost to an avid collector. Your librar-
ian can help you locate an appraiser to determine their value.

How to Get Debt Under Control

In our credit card society, it's easy for borrowing to get out of hand. The symptoms that your debt problems need to be controlled are:

- You're paying one credit card bill with a cash advance from another.
- You let bills ride from one month to the next, paying off only those that are most urgent.
- You're carrying debt in excess of 20% of your income.

If you can't seem to make any progress in reducing debts, contact one of the agencies of the non-profit National Foundation for Consumer Credit. There are more than 250 Consumer Credit Counseling Service (CCCS) agencies nationwide. If none are listed in your telephone directory, request the address of the nearest office by sending a self-addressed, stamped envelope to the National Foundation for Consumer Credit, 8701 Georgia Avenue, Silver Spring, MD 20910. These agencies provide free counseling services and will help you set up a budget and debt repayment schedule. Some companies will stop finance charges if you agree to cooperate with the CCCS repayment plan, so your debts won't keep mounting while you're trying to pay them off. According to the foundation's statistics, more than half of the people who begin a repayment program complete it successfully.

Worksheet 9: Home Equity Value

If you own your home and would consider putting its equity to work for you, complete this worksheet.

WORKSHEET 9

Can You Put Your Home Equity to Work?

---

1. Are you eligible for home equity conversion?   YES   NO

In order to qualify for home equity conversion, you must usually be age 62 or older and own and occupy free and clear (or with a small mortgage of less than 20% of your home's value) a single-family home, townhouse, or condominium. You must also live in a state that has a home equity conversion program. To find out what's available in your state, write to the AARP Home Equity Information Center, 1909 K Street NW, Washington, DC 20049.

2. Are you willing to sell your home equity to obtain a lifetime income?   YES   NO

A sale leaseback will pay you an income you can't outlive while allowing you to remain in your home. You do, however, relinquish the benefit of any future appreciation.

3. While not willing to sell your home, do you still want to draw monthly income from it for as long as you live?   YES   NO

An open-ended reverse mortgage permits you to retain property ownership indefinitely. These plans, as now designed, require that you give up the right to some or all of the future appreciation of the property. (If you want to retain both ownership and full appreciation potential, avoid shared appreciation arrangements.)

4. Do you need extra monthly income for only a limited time period, say five to ten years?   YES   NO

A fixed-term reverse mortgage pays you a monthly amount for the term you desire, normally from three to twelve years. At the end of the term, the loan must be repaid, usually from the sale of your home.

5. Do you want to be able to withdraw money only when you need it, to pay for emergency or unexpected expenses?   YES   NO

The line-of-credit reverse mortgage pemits you to make sporadic withdrawals of the amounts you need, when you need them. Repayment of the loan and accrued interest can be deferred until sale or death.

6. Do you want to stay in your home for the rest of your life?   YES   NO

Consider either a sale leaseback arrangement or a reverse mortgage that provides you with a written guarantee of lifetime occupancy.

7. Would it help you financially if you didn't have to pay property taxes each year?   YES   NO

A property tax deferral arrangement defers repayment and/or reduces the obligation (or both) until the home is sold or the owner dies.

8.   Do you need to make improvements to your home but can't afford to pay for them?   YES   NO
      A deferred payment loan arrangement helps you keep your home in shape and doesn't have to be repaid until sale or death. If you make improvements to your home—add a room or patio, for instance —these costs can be added to the original cost of your home and will eventually reduce the amount of taxable gain when the house is sold.

9.   Would a child or other relative be willing to purchase your home and then lease it back to you at a below-market rental?   YES   NO
      A sale leaseback arrangement can be structured to benefit both you and your higher tax bracket son or daughter. Check applicable Internal Revenue codes.

10.   Do you need a large sum of money to pay off debts or cover medical costs?   YES   NO
      Both the reverse mortgage and the sale leaseback arrangement can provide you with an initial disbursement of from 10% to 25% of the total loan or sale amount. You can invest this money or use it to finance fees and closing costs or pay expenses.

11.   Do you want a monthly income that keeps pace with inflation?   YES   NO
      Both the sale leaseback and the reverse mortgage may be structured so that your monthly payments increase with time.

12.   Can you locate a sponsor who will charge less than 2% to 3% of the property value to set up a sale leaseback or reverse mortgage?   YES   NO
      You'll get the greatest return on your sale leaseback or reverse mortgage by dealing with a non-profit sponsor, which will impose no or low (about 1% of the property value) fees for setting it up. For-profit sponsors, on the other hand, charge up to 4% or more of the property value, so less money goes to you.

13.   Do you want to be able to change your mind later and get your money back?   YES   NO
      If you decide later to terminate the agreement, you may be able to prepay the reverse mortgage without penalty. Sale leaseback plans, on the other hand, are difficult to reverse.

14.   Do you need cash quickly?   YES   NO
      You'll receive a reverse mortgage loan in four to six weeks, the time it takes the lender to process your application. Unless you have a ready investor, finding a buyer for a sale leaseback may take six months to a year or more.

15.   Are you eligible for a tax-free capital gain?   YES   NO
      If you (and your spouse) have lived in your home for three of the last five years, you're entitled to a once-in-a-lifetime tax-free capital gain of up to $125,000 when the house is sold. For example, a couple (age 55 or older) who purchased a home at least three years ago for $75,000 could sell it for up to $200,000 without incurring any tax liability. A sale-leaseback arrangement would allow you to extract the gain on your home (assuming neither you nor your spouse have used up the benefit in a prior sale) with minimal or no tax consequences.

HOW DO YOU SCORE?

If you answered yes to questions 2, 6, 9, 10, 11, 12, and 15, you should consider a sale leaseback arrangement. If you answered yes to questions 3, 4, 5, 6, 10, 11, 12, 13, and 14, a reverse mortgage may be a better alternative for you. If you answered yes to question 7, consider a property tax deferral arrangement. If you answered yes to question 8, look into a deferred payment loan.

For further information, a paper prepared by the staff of the Special Committee on Aging of the U.S. Senate, "Turning Home Equity into Income for Older Homeowners," discusses the various home equity conversion programs and is available from: Special Committee on Aging, U.S. Senate, G-233 Dirksen Building, Washington, DC 20510. You can also obtain sample sale-leaseback documents and several publications relating to home equity conversion, including a newsletter entitled *Home Equity News*, from: National Center for Home Equity Conversion, 110 East Main Street, Room 1010, Madison, WI 53703. Telephone 608-256-2111.

Worksheet 10:
Comparing the Costs of
Owning and Renting Your
Home

If you own your home and are thinking about selling it and then renting, complete Worksheet 10 to compare your current and future costs.

WORKSHEET 10

Should You Own or Rent Your Home?

PART I

---

1. Have you owned your home more than five years? YES NO

The percentage of your mortgage payment that is applied to your home equity rises each month, increasing more rapidly in the later years. For example, assuming you have a thirty-year mortgage at 9% and have owned your home for ten years, you've paid off only 10% of the principal amount and spent the remaining 90% on interest payments to carry the loan. After twenty years, you'll have paid almost 40% of the principal balance, and in twenty-five years nearly 65% of the principal will be repaid. Generally speaking, if you plan to live in a residence for three years or more, you're better off owning.

2. Are you able to deduct property tax payments and mortgage interest from your taxable income? YES NO

Property taxes and mortgage interest qualify as tax-deductible expenses if you have enough itemized deductions to claim them on your tax return (total itemized deductions must exceed the standard deduction in order for you to benefit from itemizing deductions—see page 121). If you don't have enough deductions, consider lumping two years' property taxes into one (if your town or county permits payment of taxes in either the current year or the following year), so that you can itemize at least every other year.

3. Are property values in your neighborhood increasing? YES NO

If property values are increasing, then your home is likely to appreciate in value, even as it grows older, making ownership more desirable. On the other hand, if you live in an area where property values are declining, your home will be worth less as time passes, and you may be better off selling it and renting.

4. Are rents in your neighborhood rising? YES NO

One of the benefits of ownership is the ability to obtain a fixed mortgage, which guarantees that your payments (principal plus interest) will stay the same from month to month. Even variable rate mortgages, which allow the lender to change the rate as interest rates rise and fall, have a cap on them, or a limit on how much you'll have to pay. In most localities, landlords can raise rents each year, so you're never certain of what your housing costs will be in the future. Be wary of special deals that promise you low rental rates the first few months or the first year. Once this low-rate term has passed, your rent may be jacked up steeply and you'll be stuck with having to pay it or incur the expenses of another move.

5. Would you consider a shared living arrangement? YES NO

Sharing your home with a friend or relative is a way to reduce both housing and living costs and enhance the pleasure of your daily life. Studies indicate that seniors who live with others stay healthier and live longer than those who live alone. If you live alone and would prefer companionship, a shared living arrangement is likely to increase both your savings and your longevity.

PART II

If three or more of your answers to the five questions in Part I are no, renting may be a better choice. Complete the calculations in Part II to compare the approximate costs of owning versus renting in the first year. You'll need your mortgage amortization schedule for determining the principal balance and the amount of interest owed for the coming year.

Your first step is to calculate the amount of equity in your home—the amount you'd end up with after paying off your mortgage (L3), brokerage commissions and other selling costs (L4), and taxes (L7). If you've made any permanent additions or improvements (not repairs or replacements), such as adding a room, garage, or swimming pool, these are also subtracted from the selling price. The amount of taxable profit (L6) is the selling price (L2) less the amount you paid (L1), less the selling costs (L4), less the value of improvements and additions (L5). If you're over 55 and have lived in the home for three of the last five years, up to $125,000 of profit from the sale of your primary residence is tax-free, if neither you nor your spouse has taken this benefit before. Otherwise, the gain will be taxable at the rate you'll compute in Chapter Eight (generally a maximum of 28%).

Your cost of owning includes mortgage interest (the principal payments increase your equity) (L9), property taxes and the difference between your annual homeowner's insurance premium and the cost of a rental policy (L10). If home values in your neighborhood are appreciating, multiply the current value of your home (L2) by the percentage increase you expect in the coming year (or the current money market rate) to determine the dollar amount of appreciation (L11). Property appreciation reduces the cost of home ownership. If you expect the value of your home to depreciate, L11 will be a negative number and increase the cost of ownership.

Your cost of renting is the annual rental you'd pay for the housing you need (L13) plus the amount of interest you'd lose on a two-month security deposit (L14), less the interest you'd earn on the invested sale proceeds from your home.

Equity in Home

    (L1) Purchase price   _____

    (L2) Current market value
(compare classified ads or obtain appraisal)   _____

    (L3) Mortgage balance
(from amortization schedule)   _____

    (L4) Selling costs
(L2 × .08)   _____

    (L5) Value of additions and improvements   _____

    (L6) Taxable profit from sale
(L2 − L1 − L4 − L5)   _____

    (L7) Capital gains tax on profit
(0 if you're entitled to once-in-a-lifetime tax-free gain, page 75;
L6 × 28% maximum or tax rate on Worksheet 15, L15)   _____

    **(L8) Your Equity in Home
(L2 − L3 − L4 − L7)**   _____

Cost of Owning

    (L9) Annual mortgage interest (from amortization schedule)   _____

    (L10) Insurance and taxes   _____

    (L11) Annual appreciation (depreciation)
(L2 × expected appreciation or money market rate)   _____

    **(L12) Cost of Owning
(L9 + L10 − L11)**   _____

Cost of Renting

    (L13) Annual rental
(check classified ads)   _____

    (L14) Interest lost on security deposit
(1/6 of L13 multiplied by money market rate)   _____

    (L15) Interest on home sale proceeds
(L8 × money market rate)   _____

    **(L16) Cost of Renting
(L13 + L14 − L15)**   _____

    **(L17) Advantage (Disadvantage) of Owning Versus Renting
(L16 − L12)**   _____

> *Sample: To Sell or Stay, That Is the Question*

Helen Jarvis's husband, Bill, died two years ago, leaving her with a home that had increased in value from $30,000 (the amount they paid eight years ago) to about $70,000, according to a recent appraisal. They had assumed a $24,000 thirty-year mortgage at 8½%, and the unpaid balance is now $22,000. When Bill was alive, he took care of most of the repairs that Helen must now pay for. Helen presently has enough money to pay expenses but is concerned that inflation will consume her savings and leave her with nothing but her home equity to fall back on. Should she sell her house to free up that money and rent instead, or should she stay where she is?

SAMPLE WORKSHEET 10 (PART II):

Should Helen Jarvis Own or Rent Her Home?

Equity in Home

(L1)	Purchase price	$30,000
(L2)	Current market value (compare classified ads or obtain appraisal)	70,000
(L3)	Mortgage balance (from amortization schedule)	22,000
(L4)	Selling costs (L2 × .08)	5,600
(L5)	Value of additions and improvements	4,500
(L6)	Taxable profit from sale (L2 − L1 − L4 −L5)	29,900
(L7)	Capital gains tax on profit (0 if you're entitled to once-in-a-lifetime tax-free gain, page 75; L6 × 28% maximum or tax rate on Worksheet 15, L15)	0
(L8)	**Your Equity in Home** (L2 − L3 − L4 − L7)	42,400

Cost of Owning

(L9)	Annual mortgage interest (from amortization schedule)	1,870
(L10)	Insurance and taxes	3,000
(L11)	Annual appreciation (depreciation) (L2 × expected appreciation or money market rate)	3,500
(L12)	**Cost of Owning** (L9 + L10 − L11)	1,370

Cost of Renting

(L13)	Annual rental (check classified ads)	6,000
(L14)	Interest lost on security deposit (1/6 of L13 multiplied by money market rate)	70

(L15) Interest on home sale proceeds
      (L8 × money market rate)

2,968

(L16) Cost of Renting
(L13 + L14 − L15)

3,102

(L17) Advantage (Disadvantage) of Owning Versus Renting
(L16 − L12)

1,732

Helen first calculates how much money she would receive if she were to sell her home at the appraised value. Selling costs (broker's commission, legal fees, and closing costs) would reduce her profit by about 8% ($5,600), increasing the cost basis (amount used for determining the taxable gain) to $35,600 ($30,000 + $5,600). Her husband had built a patio at a cost of $4,500, which further increased the cost basis to $40,100 ($35,600 + $4,500), leaving her with a net capital gain of $29,900 ($70,000 − $40,100). Since she's eligible for the once-in-a-lifetime tax-free capital gain, she would have $42,400 available to invest after paying off her mortgage ($70,000 − $22,000 − $5,600).

If Helen decided not to sell her home, her expenses of ownership would include mortgage interest ($1,870), property taxes and homeowner's insurance ($3,000). Because her neighbors have maintained their property, Helen expects the value of her house to increase by at least 5% ($3,500) next year, reducing her cost of ownership to $1,370 ($1,870 + $3,000 − $3,500 = $1,370). (If her property value actually decreased by 5%, the $3,500 would be *added* to the cost of ownership, making it $8,370).

If she were to sell her home and rent instead, her expense of annual rental on a comparable home ($6,000) plus interest lost on the two-month security deposit (⅙ of $6,000 multiplied by .07 = $70) would be partly offset by the interest she'd earn on the sale proceeds ($42,400 × .07 = $2,968). The cost of renting ($6,000 + $60 − $2,968 = $3,102) would exceed the cost of owning ($1,370) by $1,732 ($3,102 − $1,370).

Helen was happy to know that her decision to stay in her house made economic sense, because it was a better choice from an emotional standpoint as well. "I live with and care for my ailing mother," said Helen. "It's nice to have neighbors to spell me when I need to get out and shop or take some time for myself, and I'm afraid that mother's health would be worsened by a move to strange surroundings."

Helen didn't exclude the possibility of sale or home equity conversion at some future date, however. "I want to make mother as comfortable as possible while I can, but when the time comes that I'm alone, I'd like to be able to travel and do more. Then I'll either sell and move to a smaller place or consider converting the equity to cash I can use." If Helen, who's 70, were to take out a ten-year reverse mortgage today, she'd receive $292 a month for as long as she lived in the house. Since neither Helen nor her husband had ever taken the tax-free capital gain (up to $125,000) on the sale of a home that each couple over age 55 is entitled to, the profit on her home will not be subject to tax when she sells it. Two other options she should consider are deferring her property taxes and sharing her home with a compatible friend or relative, which would not only reduce each one's expenses but provide both of them with companionship and fewer household responsibilities.

Protecting Yourself From the Costs of Health Care

OBJECTIVE: To reduce health care expenses while maintaining quality. Are you health and safety conscious? Do you practice preventive medicine by eating nutritiously, exercising regularly, and thinking positively? When it comes to health insurance, is your coverage clear to you?

WHAT YOU WILL NEED

Your health insurance policies

Passage of the Medicare Catastrophic Coverage Act in 1988 will soften the financial impact of a catastrophic illness, but it does not provide coverage for long-term medical or nursing-home care, which can average between $20,000 and $35,000 a year. A Harvard University research study presented before a meeting of the U.S. House of Representatives Committee on Aging on July 30, 1985, suggests that nearly 50% of ordinarily comfortable middle-class people of age 75 who enter a private nursing home will be bankrupt in three months and more than 70% will have exhausted their resources within a year. The majority (70%) of Medicare beneficiaries have at least one supplemental health insurance policy, and many have several. The sad truth is that no one policy covers all of Medicare's gaps, and multiple policies may not pay double or triple benefits. Even if you have more than one policy, only one may pay. This means that if you're paying for more than one policy to supplement Medicare coverage, you should check to see whether you have duplicate coverage. If you do, you're not alone. It's estimated that senior citizens spend more than *$3 billion* each year on unnecessary and duplicative health insurance protection.

A survey of more than 8,000 seniors was conducted by the Subcommittee on Health and Long-Term Care of the Select Committee on Aging of the U.S. House of Representatives in 1980 and repeated in 1986. Their findings: 80% of those surveyed believed that Medicare would pay for nursing-home care if they needed it. Unfortunately, Medicare pays for less than 2% of nursing-home costs.

You can protect yourself from unnecessary and excessive health care expense by taking these two steps: the first is to do what you can to prevent accident or illness, and the second is to evaluate your insurance policies in order to minimize the costs of health protection while maximizing your protection. A wealth of practical advice on promoting good health can be found in the "Age Pages," a publication of the National Institute on Aging, which is available for $3.50 from the Superintendent of Documents, U.S. Government Printing Office, Washington, DC.

Twenty Questions and Answers About Your Health Protection

1. When do you become eligible for Medicare benefits?

Medicare consists of two parts—hospital insurance (Part A) and medical insurance (Part B). Hospital insurance helps pay for in-patient hospital care and certain follow-up care. You become eligible for hospital insurance at age 65 if you are entitled to monthly Social Security or railroad retirement benefits. You're eligible before age 65 if you've been entitled to Social Security disability benefits for twenty-four months or if you meet the requirements of the Social Security disability program. Almost anyone who is 65 or older is eligible for medical insurance. (If you're under 65 but over 50, you can become a member of the American Association of Retired Persons [AARP, 1909 K Street NW, Washington, DC 20049], which provides health insurance benefits through Prudential Insurance Company after a three-month waiting period for existing conditions.)

2. Will your Medicare benefits begin automatically at age 65?

When you reach age 65 and apply for Social Security benefits, hospital insurance protection will start automatically. Medical insurance protection (Part B), at a basic premium of $24.80/month (in 1988) also will begin automatically unless you say you don't want it. The monthly premium is deducted from your Social Security benefit. If you continue to work after age 65 and have employer's health insurance, Medicare will act as a supplement to your employer plan. You or your doctor should file a claim first with the employer plan. If the employer doesn't pay in full, a claim should be sent to Medicare for supplemental payment.

3. When should you cancel your present health insurance?

Discuss your situation with your insurance agent or the benefits counselor where you work, particularly if your present policy covers your dependents. In any case, do not cancel any health insurance until the month your Medicare coverage begins.

4. What can you expect Medicare hospital insurance to pay for?

Medicare doesn't pay the entire cost for all covered services. The part that you pay is called the deductible (the initial amount). If you're admitted to a hospital, Medicare will pay for all covered services after a deductible of $564 (in 1989).

5. What hospital services will Medicare cover?

Covered services include semi-private room, meals, regular nursing care, operating and recovery room costs, hospital costs for anesthesia, intensive and coronary care, drugs, laboratory tests, X rays, medical supplies and appliances, and rehabilitation services.

6. Will you be covered if you require continuing care after you leave the hospital?

Medicare will help pay for up to 150 days in a nursing facility per benefit period. You pay 20% of the costs for the first eight days and Medicare pays all costs for the next 142 days. No prior hospitalization is required for you to qualify. If you're confined to your home, it will pay the full cost of an unlimited number of home visits by a health agency, provided your condition fulfills *all* the criteria for payment. The requirements for skilled nursing facility coverage under Medicare Part A are extremely restrictive. Therefore, most nursing-home residents receive little or no Medicare coverage. Rarely do individuals qualify for the full 150 days of post-hospital, extended-care services available as a benefit under Part A. If care is provided by a Medicare-certified hospice, Medicare will pay for a maximum of 210 days, unless the physician or hospice director recertifies that the individual is still terminally ill.

7. What can you expect Medicare medical insurance (Part B) to pay for?

After meeting the annual medical insurance deductible ($75 in 1988), Part B pays 80% of the "Medicare approved amount" of doctors' services, medical services, and supplies that are not covered by hospital insurance (including most services needed by people with permanent kidney failure). Covered doctors' services include surgical services, diagnostic tests and X rays, office medical care and treatment, and hospital out-patient diagnosis and treatment. Part B can also cover ambulance transportation, home dialysis, oral surgery, speech, radiation, and physical therapy. Doctors who "take Medicare" accept Medicare's approved amount as full payment and cannot legally bill you for more. You're billed only for 20% of the "approved amount" (co-payment). Where the health care provider does not take Medicare assignment, Medicare pays 80% of a "reasonable" charge. Thus, if a doctor charges $120 for a service for which Medicare says the reasonable charge is $100, Medicare pays $80 (80% of $100) and the patient must pay the $40 difference. Beginning January 1, 1990, no one will have to pay more than $1,370 annually for Medicare-approved expenses. Also starting in 1990, Medicare will pay 75% of the cost of home intravenous and immunosuppressive drugs used the first year following a transplant, after a $550 deductible. In 1991, it will pay 50% of the cost of *all* prescription drugs, after a $600 deductible, and in 1992 it will pay 60% of the cost after a $652 deductible. Individuals who have exceeded the $1,370 limit or the prescription drug deductible and who require assistance with daily activities such as eating, bathing, and dressing are eligible for up to 80 hours a year of respite care —the services of a nurse or health aide to care for them at home.

8.   What will the expanded Medicare benefits cost you?

The cost of this legislation is being paid for by those who are eligible for Medicare. You'll pay in two ways. First, $4 a month ($48 a year) is deducted from your Social Security check in 1989 to help fund the program. This deduction increases annually to $10.20 a month ($122.40 a year) in 1993. Second, beginning with your 1989 income tax return (due April 15, 1990) you'll have to pay a surcharge to the IRS if you are over age 65 and have $10,000 a year or more in taxable income. The surcharge for individuals rises annually from 15% of the amount over $10,000 (capped at $800) in 1989 to 28% with a $1,050 cap in 1993. A married couple pays approximately twice this amount.

9.   What health care expenses are not covered by Medicare?

Medicare does not pay for dental care; eye, ear, and foot care; out-of-hospital prescription drugs and medications (until 1990); and routine physical checkups. Most important, Medicare does not cover the most devastating expense—custodial and "intermediate" level nursing and home care beyond the first hundred days. (At this writing,

Congress is considering legislation that would appropriate federal funds to offset some of these expenses.)

10. If you are employed and covered by a group health insurance plan, will it supplement Medicare protection after you retire?

In the past, many employers made post-retirement continuation of major medical health coverage a part of their employee benefits package. If you are protected by such coverage, it can be one of the best ways to supplement Medicare benefits.

11. If you're not employed, how can you protect yourself from the health care costs not covered by Medicare?

You can select a doctor who is willing to accept assignment of Medicare benefits. Doctors do not have to accept assignment, but many do. You can purchase a health insurance policy that will pay for some of those costs not covered by Medicare insurance, a so-called medigap policy. You can also enroll in a Health Maintenance Organization (HMO). HMOs provide both insurance and medical and hospital services. You pay an annual membership fee and receive health care services (some of which aren't covered by Medicare) at no additional cost. The HMO is directly reimbursed by Medicare for covered services.

12. What expenses can you expect a medigap policy to pay for?

In general, an insurance policy officially licensed by a state as a medigap policy must meet minimum standards, which include payment of the Medicare deductibles and co-payments that, beginning in 1989, consist of the first $564 and $1,370 of hospital and doctors' costs each year, not enough of an expense to warrant their $500 to $900 annual premium cost unless additional benefits are offered. *All* medigap policies will change as a result of the new legislation. Insurers are examining and redesigning their products to fill in some of the Medicare gaps that still remain, such as doctors' charges in excess of the "reasonable" amount, the prescription drug costs not covered by Medicare, and the cost of home-health and nursing home care. If you currently have a medigap policy, its provisions and benefits will change in 1989 and you should determine whether they are worth the premium cost.

13. Can you cover all the gaps in Medicare by purchasing more than one medigap policy?

No, you can't. If you purchase more than one supplemental policy, you will probably be duplicating some coverage, while still being at risk.

14. How can you select a medigap policy?

Generally, medigap group policies that are offered by major, well-known insurance companies are well thought of. If you're still employed, your group plan may be the best protection because it has no waiting period before it becomes effective and doesn't exclude pre-existing conditions. Before buying any coverage, ask the agent for literature showing the company rated A or A+ by A. M. Best Co.'s rating service and compare the policy with medigap insurance offered through Blue Cross–Blue Shield, which is often the best protection on a dollar-for-dollar basis.

15. What medigap policies should you avoid?

Avoid individual policies, particularly those offered by companies whose names are unfamiliar to you. Many of these are not medigap policies and do not meet minimum standards. In particular, steer clear of policies that are sold door to door or on television or appear to be government sponsored. Advertising materials that display the federal eagle or resemble official government documents are designed to deceive you. Avoid any policy that pays benefits only for specific ailments, such as cancer or heart disease. Their benefits tend to be extremely modest compared to the costs you would actually incur if you contracted any of those diseases. Avoid "hospital indemnity" policies, or any other policy (except for Medicare and Medicare supplement) that pays you only if you're hospitalized. The average hospital stay is less than ten days, so that the amount of benefits you would be likely to receive is modest. State insurance departments approve policies, but this only means that the company and policy meet the state's legal requirements, not that they are state sponsored. Refuse to purchase insurance from agents who use high-pressure sales tactics or who represent themselves as federal employees. Report any suspicious practices to your state insurance department.

16. Are there any specific policy provisions to look for?

Before you purchase any policy, read it carefully and complete the application accurately, giving all requested information about your health history. You should receive a clearly worded outline of the policy provisions. Avoid policies that will not cover current or previous health conditions and those that exclude coverage of existing conditions for a period of more than six months from the date of purchase. The best policies will begin covering existing health problems within three months, but these are more costly. If the policy states that no medical examination is required, you may not be protected should a pre-existing condition recur. If an agent tries to convince you to give up your present coverage, you may be trading insurance that covers your pre-existing health problems for insurance that doesn't. Be certain that you have the right to renew coverage. Group policies that are guaranteed renewable can't cancel protection unless they cancel all the policies of the same type, so they can't single you out and terminate your coverage because of a claim or dispute. Policies that are automatically renewable or guaranteed renewable for life offer added protection.

17. What if you change your mind after you've bought a policy?

If you decide to buy a policy, choose one that allows you to review it for ten days (some allow thirty days), during which time you can receive a refund of your premium. Don't pay cash, and make your check payable to the insurance company, not the agent.

18. What should you consider before enrolling in a Health Maintenance Organization (HMO) or signing up with another health care provider?

Joining an HMO is like doing all your shopping at one store. If it offers everything you want, it can be a good deal for you. For a flat fee, the HMO may cover all Medicare deductibles and co-payments with no limit on the hospitalization period. Services that aren't covered by Medicare, such as eye and hearing examinations, may be available at minimal cost. As an HMO member you'll have no insurance claim forms to complete, and you may find it easier to stay within a strict budget because you'll know exactly how much your health care will cost each month. The main drawback to an HMO is that you must use the physicians and hospital facilities they provide. Before you sign up with an HMO, visit the facility and ask members if they've been happy with their treatment and whether they have any complaints. Find out, also, if there's an affiliation with a teaching hospital that's equipped to handle complex procedures such as open heart surgery. Then ask the state office that regulates HMOs whether the one you're considering is in sound financial condition. More than twenty-five HMOs have gone out of business because of financial mismanagement, leaving their patients with unpaid bills. You can obtain additional information on HMOs from: Group Health Association of America, 1129 20th Street NW, Suite 600, Washington, DC 20036.

19. What if you can't afford to pay for extra insurance?

If you have a low income and few assets other than your home, you may qualify for Medicaid. Medicaid pays almost all health care costs, including long-term nursing care. Contact your local social service agency to find out if you qualify and to determine what the benefits are in your state.

20. Where can you obtain additional free information on Medicare and supplemental Medicare insurance?

Call you local Social Security office if you have any specific questions. You should also ask them to send you these publications: "Your Medicare Handbook" (Publication #HCFA-10050), "What You Should Know About Medicare" (SSA Publication #05-10043), and "Guide to Health Insurance for People with Medicare" (Publication #HCFA 02110). Many states provide free booklets and information, which you can receive by calling or writing your state insurance commissioner's office.

> *How Can You Pay the Costs of Long-Term Nursing-Home Care for Yourself or Your Spouse?*

The need for nursing-home care over a long period of time is one of the major financial risks of aging that cannot be met by any kind of conventional planning. About 6% of Americans aged 75 to 85 are in nursing homes. The number rises to 25% in the over-85 age group—a group that is expected to rise from its present (1988) 3 million to 5.1 million by the year 2000.

If you or your spouse seem likely to require long-term nursing-home care, or if you fear that possibility, then you should review the protection you currently have and see what else you can do to protect yourself.

As noted above, *Medicare* coverage for nursing-home costs is extremely limited. At its best, it pays only part of the costs for only 150 days at a time and is subject to a number of strict conditions. The result is that Medicare pays for only a fraction of all nursing-home costs in the United States.

Nursing-home insurance is a relatively new type of long-term health care insurance that covers most nursing-home costs. Policies are offered by more than seventy companies, including Aetna, American Express, AIG Life, CNA, and Prudential. Generally, they pay $30 to $100 a day for two to six years in a nursing home. Many policies do not cover pre-existing conditions or home health care. Depending on age and the amount of coverage, annual premiums on a guaranteed renewable policy range from about $300 to well over $1,000. An American Express policy, for example, offers holders the choice of receiving from $10 to $80 a day for nursing-home care. An Amex policy that pays $60 a day ($21,900/year) for four years (excluding the first twenty days) costs someone under 60 years of age $450 a year; people from 60 to 64 pay $540 a year; those from 65 to 69 pay $720; a 75-year-old would pay $1,044 a year; and an 80-year-old, $1,404. After the companies issue a policy, they generally guarantee that the premium will stay the same irrespective of advancing age or changing health (with the exception of across-the-board premium increases for all policyholders in a state). If the policyholder leaves the nursing home after 180 days, the typical policy pays half the daily benefit for at-home care.

Before considering such a policy, inquire about the following points:

- Does the policy cover not just skilled care, including physical therapy or other highly trained care, but also custodial care that includes meals and help with medications?
- Are the daily benefits adequate and does the policy cover regular home health care as well as nursing-home care?
- Does the policy require that the nursing-home admission be preceded by a hospital stay?
- How many days must elapse before benefits start?
- For how many days or years will benefits be paid?
- Does the policy bar coverage for certain conditions?
- What happens to your coverage if you move to another state?

For a list of insurers selling long-term-care policies in your state, contact the Health Insurance Association of America, 1001 Pennsylvania Avenue NW, Washington, DC 20004. The May 1988 issue of *Consumer Reports* includes a comprehensive evaluation of long-term-care policies and rates fifty-three insurance underwriters. For a copy, send $3 to: Reprints/Consumer Reports, P.O. Box 53016, Boulder, CO 80322.

Medicaid is a joint federal-state health care program that is administered by local governments for people who cannot pay their medical expenses. It can make a vast difference in your welfare if your spouse is already in a nursing home or is expected to require nursing-home care in the future because of a chronic or untreatable condition such as Alzheimer's disease. To qualify for Medicaid once in a nursing home, your spouse must have a modest level of assets—approximately $12,000, the exact amount varying from state to state—and medical costs that take most or all of his or her income. (Your assets and income will not be considered available to your spouse after he or she has moved out of the home you lived in together and been in a nursing home for a certain waiting period—one to six months, depending on your state.) Of course, no one can merely give away assets in order to qualify for Medicaid. There are waiting periods and, in some situations, penalty periods for certain kinds of transfers. However, there are a number of appropriate things that you and your spouse can do to advance the date of your spouse's eligibility for Medicaid.

The benefit of Medicaid is that it reduces, but does not eliminate, the cost to you of providing nursing-home care for your spouse. A spouse who qualifies for Medicaid is required to pay the nursing home an amount slightly less than his or her monthly income from Social Security, other public or private pension, and any other source. Neither you nor your spouse nor any relative is required to pay any additional amount. The state Medicaid agency will pay the nursing home an additional amount so that the total paid will equal what is called the Medicaid reimbursement amount. This is significantly less than what you would pay as a private patient.

Your goal, then, when your spouse is already in a nursing home or is reasonably likely to require nursing home care, is to reduce your spouse's assets as quickly as possible, following the rules with respect to what is permitted by Medicaid. If you do not know which of you is likely to require nursing home care, or if you are already a surviving spouse, these rules apply equally but are less useful in planning what to do. You should consult an expert on Medicaid in your state to determine what steps, if any, you should take. The following rules apply in many but not all states; they may give you an idea of what your choices are.

1. *The home is "exempt."* The home in which you and your spouse lived will not be considered an asset of your spouse for determining Medicaid eligibility so long as you or a dependent child is living in it.

2. *Thirty-month transfer rule, with exceptions.* In general, anything that your spouse gives away in the thirty months prior to applying for Medicaid counts as an asset in determining eligibility for Medicaid. Thus, if your spouse gave you $20,000 today, he or she would have to report that amount as an asset on a Medicaid application filed any time within the next thirty months, after which, under most states' rules, it would no longer count as your spouse's asset. Following are some important exceptions to the thirty-month wait rule:

a. Your spouse can give you his or her interest in your home so long as your spouse, you, or a dependent relative is living in it, without adversely affecting Medicaid eligibility.

b. If you and your spouse evenly divide a jointly owned asset, such as a bank account or stock, the half that you take for yourself will not count as an asset of your spouse in determining Medicaid eligibility.

c. If you or another co-owner take money out of your spouse's bank account, in some states that will not count as a "transfer" by your spouse and will not adversely affect Medicaid eligibility.

d. Your spouse can pay children or other relatives (but not you) for providing care and assistance, and it will not be considered a transfer so long as it is done under a written contract. (However, all of those payments are income to the person who receives them and should be reported on their federal and state income tax returns.)

Because specific requirements for Medicaid eligibility vary from state to state and are extremely complicated, no reorganization of assets should be undertaken without first consulting someone who is an expert on your state's Medicaid rules. You may be able to locate an attorney who has expertise in this area through your local Legal Aid office or Area Agency on Aging.

Legislation has been introduced that would help pay for long-term health care costs. Bills in the Senate would cover custodial nursing-home care and Representative Claude Pepper (D-Fla.) sponsored a bill that would be funded through new payroll taxes and would provide up to $2,045 in monthly home health care benefits. Although the bill was defeated in June 1988, it's likely that Congress will continue to be faced with the issue until a solution is found.

The United Seniors Health Cooperative's publication "Long-Term Care: A Dollar and Sense Guide" discusses the options available for paying for physical, medical, and other support often needed in life. To obtain a copy, send $6.95 to: USHC, 1334 G Street NW, Suite 500, Washington, DC 20005.

Worksheet 11: Comparison Shopping for Health Insurance	Compare the provisions of the policies you now own and those you're considering.

WORKSHEET 11

Compare Before You Buy

	Benefit Period	Medicare Pays (1988)	Medicare Pays (1989)	All Medigap Policies Pay At Least (1988)	Your Policy Pays
Hospitalization (Part A)					
Semiprivate room & board.	First 60 days	All but $540	All but $564; no limit to coverage	May pay $540	_____
Hospital services & supplies: meals, drugs, special care, diagnostic X rays, lab tests, operating and recovery rooms	61–91 days	All but $135/day		$135/day	_____
	Beyond 91 days	All but $270/day for 60 days		$270/day for 60 days	_____
Skilled nursing facility care in a Medicare-approved facility (you must have been in hospital at least three days prior to entering facility in the last thirty days)	First 20 days	100%	80% of costs for first 8 days; 100% of costs for next 142 days; nothing beyond 150 days; no prior hospitalization required		_____
	21–100 days	All but $67.50/day		$67.50/day	_____
	Beyond 100 days	Nothing		100%	_____
Medical Expenses (Part B)					
Services of a physician, speech or physical therapist, use of ambulance, tests administered by physician, medical supplies (excluding prescribed medicine)		80% of approved charges after annual $75 deductible	Beginning January 1, 1990: 80% of approved charges after annual $75 deductible; all costs after patient has paid $1370; part of prescription drug costs	May pay $75 or $125 deductible; 20% of Medicare-eligible expenses after $200 annual deductible to an annual maximum of $5,000	_____ _____ _____

1. What is the annual premium? _____

2. Can you get a refund of your premium if you change your mind in 10 days? _____

3. Is the policy automatically renewable or guaranteed renewable for life? Other? _____

4. Will the policy pay for a second medical opinion if surgery is recommended? _____

5. What is the exclusion period for pre-existing conditions? _____

6. Will the policy pay for any extras, such as eye or ear care? _____

CHAPTER 7

Protecting Yourself From Hazards at Home and Away

OBJECTIVE: To reduce the costs of your home and automobile insurance coverage without sacrificing necessary protection. What can you do to recover losses resulting from theft or casualty?

WHAT YOU WILL NEED
> Home and automobile insurance policies
> Home mortgage amortization schedule
> Contents of wallet and safe deposit box

As you get older, safety becomes a greater concern. Accidents are likely to be more frequent and more serious in later life. Poor eyesight and loss of hearing decrease your awareness of the hazards that surround you. Arthritis and neurological disorders can make you less steady on your feet. Medications can dull your reflexes and lengthen your response time. If you do fall or suffer an injury, it will take longer to heal than it did when you were young.

Many accidents are preventable. Falls—the number one cause of fatal injury in the aged—can be prevented by taking simple precautions and making your surroundings as safe as possible. According to the U.S. Consumer Product Safety Commission (CPSC), many home accidents result from hazards that are easy to overlook but also easy to fix. Obtain a free copy of their home safety checklist, "Safety for Older Consumers," by calling 1-800-638-2772 or writing U.S. Consumer Product Safety Commission, Washington, DC 20207.

**Reducing Property
Insurance Expenses**

Even though your home and car may be as safe as you can make them, they're still obstacles to your financial security. Storm damage or burglary can cost you thousands of dollars. Even worse, if someone is injured in your home or as a result of an automobile accident caused by you, you may be sued for a large sum of money and involved in a lengthy, grueling legal proceeding. How can you protect yourself from such a disaster? By buying insurance. The purpose of insurance is to protect you from the major losses, the catastrophes that could cost you many thousands or even millions of dollars. The cost of home and automobile insurance can be greatly reduced by using it only to protect yourself from large losses and by absorbing the small losses. The deductible amount—the dollar amount of damage you're willing to assume before your insurance company enters the picture—plays a major role in determining how much your proection will cost.

Most insurance policies are written in legal language that's difficult to understand and interpret. Many commonly used insurance terms do not really mean what they say. All-risk property insurance, for example, doesn't cover all risks (it covers all *insurable* risks; natural disasters such as floods aren't considered insurable), and comprehensive automobile protection is not truly comprehensive (it doesn't cover collision damage or liability for injuries to others).

**Worksheets 12 and 13:
Evaluating Present Levels
of Insurance Protection**

Review your policy provisions so that you can answer these questions correctly. If you have difficulty understanding the policy language, call your agent for a translation. You should understand your policy and know the kind and amount of coverage you need so that you can reduce your insurance premiums and put the money you save to work for you instead.

WORKSHEET 12

Evaluate Your Home Insurance Protection

---

1. If you own a home, there are four types of policies: HO-1 covers damage by fire, lightning, hail, windstorm, explosion, riot, aircraft, vehicles, and smoke, vandalism and theft; HO-2 (called the "broad form") covers the additional perils of damage caused by falling objects, the weight of snow, building collapse, overheated or freezing water pipes, and electrical accidents; HO-3 (called the "special") adds to the broad form coverage damage caused by spilled paint, water and oil leakage, wild animals, and guests. HO-8 covers older homes with hard-to-replace special features. None cover damage due to floods, earthquake, war, nuclear accident, or wear and tear. Because the risks covered by HO-3 are unlikely, HO-1 or the broad form (HO-2) are your best buy. If you rent or live in a condominium, HO-4 and HO-6 provide broad form protection (see chart on page 103).

What type of policy do you need?   _____

2. If you live in an area where floods or earthquakes occur, you may be able to purchase insurance protection, which must be in effect at least five days before damage occurs. You can reduce your annual premium by increasing the deductible (the dollar amount of damage you pay for before insurance goes into effect) to $1,000 or more. To find out if your community is covered by flood insurance, call 1-800-638-6620.

Should you buy flood or earthquake insurance?   YES   NO

3. Your residence (exclusive of the land value) must be insured for 80% of its replacement cost (not its original cost, which may be far less) in order for you to be fully reimbursed for damages. Inflation-guard policies that increase your coverage at regular intervals still do not guarantee full protection. If your home has appreciated sharply since you bought it, check with your agent to make sure you're adequately covered.

If your home is damaged, will your insurance company restore it to
its original condition?   YES   NO

4. Standard policies insure a structure's contents for 50% of the amount of coverage on the structure, less a deductible of $250. However, each item is considered to be depreciated for valuation purposes, so the amount received will be less than the cost to replace it. The money you save by increasing the deductible to $500 or $1,000 will pay for a replacement cost policy, which will reimburse you for the full repurchase price, whatever it may be.

Will you be adequately compensated for loss or damage to the contents
of your home?   YES   NO

5. Insurance companies encourage policymakers to add protection by offering premium discounts. You may be able to reduce your premiums by 15% or more if you purchase fire extinguishers and install smoke detectors, dead-bolt locks, and a home security system.

Will making your home safer reduce your insurance premiums?   YES   NO

6. Most policies limit coverage on valuable personal property. The limits typically are: $100 for total amount of cash and coins; $500 for total value of jewelry and furs; $1,000 for total value of silverware. You'll need a Personal Articles Floater policy (cost about $60 a year per $5,000 coverage) to cover specific items. If you don't use the items and don't want to pay the cost of protection, store them in a safe deposit box.

Will your insurance cover your valuables?   YES   NO

7. Liability protection is the most important provision of your homeowners' policy. A fall or other injury incurred by someone while in your home or on your property could result in a lawsuit costing many thousand dollars. For less than $100 a year you can purchase an umbrella liability policy that will tack $1 million or more of insurance protection on to your basic home and auto liability policies. In order to purchase an umbrella policy, you'll need a minimum of $50,000 in liability protection under your home policy.

Are you adequately protected if someone sues you for injuries or damages incurred on your property?   YES   NO

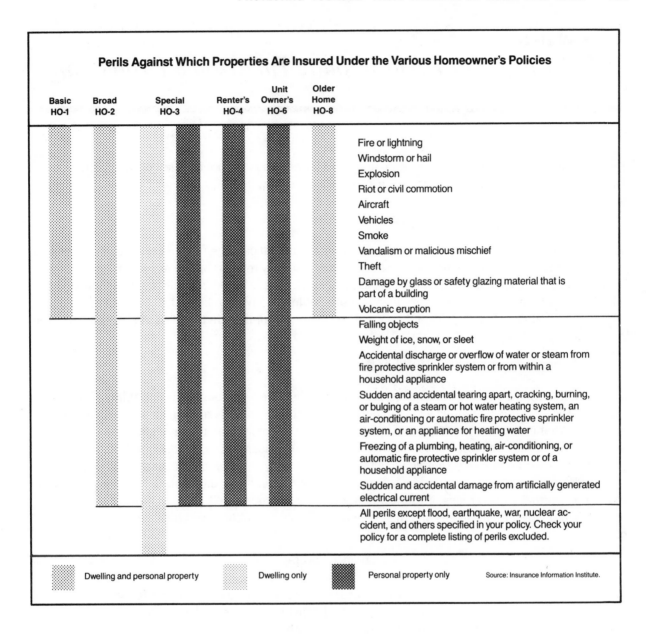

Perils Against Which Properties Are Insured Under the Various Homeowner's Policies

Basic HO-1	Broad HO-2	Special HO-3	Renter's HO-4	Unit Owner's HO-6	Older Home HO-8	
						Fire or lightning
						Windstorm or hail
						Explosion
						Riot or civil commotion
						Aircraft
						Vehicles
						Smoke
						Vandalism or malicious mischief
						Theft
						Damage by glass or safety glazing material that is part of a building
						Volcanic eruption
						Falling objects
						Weight of ice, snow, or sleet
						Accidental discharge or overflow of water or steam from fire protective sprinkler system or from within a household appliance
						Sudden and accidental tearing apart, cracking, burning, or bulging of a steam or hot water heating system, an air-conditioning or automatic fire protective sprinkler system, or an appliance for heating water
						Freezing of a plumbing, heating, air-conditioning, or automatic fire protective sprinkler system or of a household appliance
						Sudden and accidental damage from artificially generated electrical current
						All perils except flood, earthquake, war, nuclear accident, and others specified in your policy. Check your policy for a complete listing of perils excluded.

Dwelling and personal property   Dwelling only   Personal property only   Source: Insurance Information Institute.

WORSHEET 13
Evaluate Your Automobile Insurance Protection

There are several components to your automobile policy and you may not need all of them. The following questions will help you determine which are necessary.

1. Collision insurance reimburses you for repair of accidental damage to your car, regardless of who is at fault. You can sharply reduce the cost of this protection by requesting the maximum deductible. For example, if you're willing to pay the first $1,000 of damage incurred in a mishap, your collision premium may be as much as 50% less than if you're willing to pay only the first $100. You may not need this protection at all. If your car is worth $2,500 or less (or is more than five or six years old), you should consider dropping this coverage.

Can you reduce your collision insurance premiums?　　　　　　　　　YES　　　NO

2. Comprehensive auto insurance isn't really "comprehensive"—it doesn't cover liability for accidents caused by you nor does it protect you from uninsured motorists or medical expenses resulting from an accident. What it does cover is the cost of repairing damages other than those arising from an accident. These include theft, vandalism, and natural causes such as fire, windstorm, flood, and earthquake. You can reduce your premiums for this portion of your coverage the same way you reduce your collision insurance premiums—by assuming a large deductible or eliminating coverage entirely if your car is worth $2,500 or less. If your car is worth more but you keep it garaged most of the time where it's protected from vandals and the elements, you can probably do without comprehensive coverage.

Can you reduce your comprehensive insurance coverage?　　　　　　　YES　　　NO

3. Your health insurance policy pays for the cost of medical care to you and your family, regardless of the cause. There is no benefit to carrying additional medical insurance, because you will not receive duplicate benefits (you'll collect from one insurer or the other, but not both). However, you should consider carrying $5,000 coverage for non-related passengers.

Do you need insurance to cover the cost of medical care required as the result of an automobile accident?　　　　　　　　　　　　　　　　　　　　　　　　　　YES　　　NO

4. Many states have no-fault laws, which require you to receive compensation of up to a certain amount (say $10,000) from your own insurance company, regardless of who caused the accident. This protection is provided by the liability portion of your insurance policy. You must purchase uninsured and underinsured motorists coverage if you do not reside in a no-fault state ($50,000 should be sufficient) or if you desire additional protection ($50,000 minus your state's no-fault limit).

If you're involved in an accident caused by a driver who has little or no insurance, do you need protection?　　　　　　　　　　　　　　　　　　　　　　　　　　　　YES　　　NO

5. You must be protected against the costs that may result from an accident caused by you. The legal system has granted awards of millions of dollars to individuals and families who suffered injuries or loss of life and property as the result of an accident. If you carry a limit of $300,000 bodily injury and property damage liability, you qualify for umbrella liability protection, which covers both your home and your auto for $1 million or more and can cost less than $100. (If your net worth is less than $200,000, you don't need this extra protection.) If your insurance company separates coverage for bodily injury liability from property damage liability, $25,000 protection for damage to the property of others is sufficient.

Do you have adequate protection from legal actions arising out of an accident caused by you or your spouse?   YES   NO

6. Because premiums can vary from one company to another by as much as 50%, it's worth your while to spend some time shopping for automobile insurance. As a basis for comparison, check the rates charged by State Farm, the country's largest insurance agency and one of the lowest in cost. Two other low-cost insurers are Amica Mutual (401-521-9100) and USAA (800-531-8000), which insures retired commissioned armed services personnel. Find out whether the company has agents in your locality who can expedite your claims.

Which insurance company should you use?   _____

7. The liability portion of your policy protects you when you're driving someone else's car and when they're driving your car. In short, both you and your car are protected. If you have an accident while driving someone else's car, however, your collision policy will not cover the costs of repair.

Are you covered if you share driving with a neighbor or relative, in their car or yours?   YES   NO

8. Check with insurers to find out how much you can save if you qualify for the following discounts: senior citizen, non-smoker, anti-theft devices installed, safe driving record (both you and spouse), no drivers under age 25 in household, car kept in garage. If you're considering purchasing a car, you can reduce your insurance premium by 30% or more by buying a model that's likely to suffer less damage in an accident, costs less to repair, and is less likely to be stolen than the average car in that price range. Check with insurers for a current list of lower-premium autos before you buy. It could save both your money and your life.

Are you taking advantage of all the ways to lower your insurance premiums, in addition to those listed above?   YES   NO

9. If your accident record is making it difficult for you to find an insurance company that's willing to protect you, perhaps you should investigate another means of travel such as bus, train, or taxi. If public transportation is inconvenient or unavailable in your vicinity, consider an arrangement with a neighbor or relative who will provide transportation in exchange for money or a service you can offer. If you must drive, compare the rates of substandard companies with those that provide coverage under an assigned risk plan (the assigned risk is often less costly). If you've been turned down for coverage for reasons other than being involved in an accident and you live in Hawaii, Massachusetts, Michigan, New Hampshire, North Carolina, or South Carolina, you are guaranteed the right to buy insurance from any company you choose.

Have you considered other methods of transportation?   YES   NO

Worksheet 14:
Your Household, Wallet,
and Safe Deposit Box
Inventories

Insurance claims people say that the average theft or fire victim can't remember more than half of the items that were in the home before the tragedy. Test the validity of this statement by listing the contents of one of your rooms without looking first. Try the same test on the contents of your wallet. Then score yourself to see how you did. Did you include draperies, pictures, carpets, and accessories? Did you include all of your credit cards and remember how much cash you had? If you left some items off your lists now, when you're relaxed and thinking clearly, imagine how poorly you'd do following a casualty. Why tax your memory skills when you can quickly and easily make a list of your personal assets and valuables? Along with your household inventory, you'll need purchase receipts and property appraisals (for valuables) to document losses for prompt payment of claims and to substantiate the loss deduction on your tax return.

WORKSHEET 14

Your Household and Personal Inventory

ROOM _____

Article Description	Date of Purchase	Purchase Price	Location of Receipt/Warranty

To further avoid any problems in determining the worth of your belongings, take snapshots of the contents of each room. Store photographs of the contents of each room, along with Worksheet 14, in your safe deposit box (consider having one box for each spouse), or give duplicate photos and a copy of the worksheet to a trusted friend or relative.

WALLET AND CREDIT CARD INVENTORY

Name of User	Card Number	Expiration Date	Telephone Number

Other Contents of Wallet: _____

SAFE DEPOSIT BOX INVENTORY

Your safe deposit box should contain:

Stock and bond certificates
Mortgage notes
Business agreements
Birth certificates
Marriage and divorce records
Citizenship papers and passports
Military records
Deeds and property appraisals
Automobile titles
Valuables such as coins, stamps, and precious jewelry

Location of Box _____

Box Number _____ Who has keys? _____

Description of Items

_____

_____

_____

_____

_____

_____

_____

_____

_____

_____

_____

_____

_____

_____

_____

CHAPTER 8

Reduce Your Income Taxes

OBJECTIVE: To minimize your federal income tax liability. Which is the best filing status for you? What can you do to lower your taxes? How much do taxes reduce your investment return? Will you owe taxes on your Social Security benefits? What is the financial impact of divorce?

WHAT YOU WILL NEED

Your most recent federal income tax return

Beginning in 1987, the most far-reaching tax legislation in several decades went into effect. The changes are being implemented gradually over a four-year period and are likely to affect every senior citizen. The money you save by legally reducing your taxes is money that you can put to work for you. Now that you've taken the time to sort out and organize your financial affairs, you'll easily be able to keep track of tax deductibles and time your expenditures to minimize or eliminate your tax liability.

How the Tax Law Works

The most important change effected by the 1986 tax reform was the simplification of tax brackets. For years prior to 1987, your income could be progressively taxed at as many as fifteen different rates, depending upon how much you earned. For example, if you were single and earned a taxable income of $13,000, some of your income was taxed at 11%, some at 12%, 14%, and 15%, and your last dollar of income was taxed at 18%. Your highest ("marginal") rate of 18% applied to any earnings up to the next level of $14,660. The higher your marginal rate, the more valuable your deductions.

The Tax Reform Act of 1986 created five tax rates for 1987 and three rates (for most people) in 1988 and thereafter. In 1988, the highest (marginal) tax rate for a single person earning a taxable income of $13,000 is 15%, lower than the 18% rate of 1986. However, *all* net taxable income is taxed at that rate, not just part of it. The result: your tax bill in 1986 on $13,000 of net taxable income was $1,500; in 1988 it increased to $1,950.

This tax rate increase was offset, however, by an increase in the value of *personal exemptions* and the *standard deduction*, to result in a lower tax for most senior citizens. Prior to 1987, each individual was allowed one personal exemption (valued at $1,080) and an additional personal exemption for being blind or over 65. In 1986, a 75-year-old blind couple—call them Mr. and Mrs. Boone—could take six personal exemptions, reducing their taxable income by a total of $6,480 ($1,080 × 6). They could also take a standard deduction of $3,670 ($2,480 for single filers).

The tax reform increased the value of the personal exemption (from $1,080 to $1,900 in 1987, $1,950 in 1988, $2,000 in 1989, and adjusted for inflation thereafter), but eliminated the additional personal exemptions for the blind and those over 65. In 1988, the Boones are entitled to two personal exemptions, reducing their taxable income by a total of $3,900 (versus $6,480 in 1986 and $3,800 in 1987).

Congress also added a special standard deduction for those blind or over 65 and increased the value of the standard deduction for everyone. In 1987 and 1988, a married couple age 65 or older is entitled to a standard deduction of $5,000 plus $600 ($750 for a single person) for those who are blind. The Boones' *standard deduction* is $7,400 in 1987 and 1988 versus $3,670 in 1986.

Most low- and middle-income families who don't itemize deductions will come out ahead with this tax reform. Those who were able to itemize before will not benefit from itemizing deductions unless they exceed the value of the standard deduction. The Boones' itemized deductions, for example, would have to exceed $7,400 in 1987 and 1988 —more than half their taxable income—in order for them to further reduce their taxes.

How Does Tax Reform Affect You?

Because Social Security benefits are generally not taxable, most low- to middle-income seniors are likely to pay less tax than they did in prior years and less than younger people who earn the same amount of fully taxable income. Here is how your income and expenses are calculated for tax purposes.

GROSS TAXABLE INCOME

minus

ADJUSTMENTS

equals

ADJUSTED GROSS INCOME (AGI)

minus

the greater of:

ITEMIZED DEDUCTIONS or THE STANDARD DEDUCTION

minus

PERSONAL EXEMPTIONS

equals

NET TAXABLE INCOME

COMPUTE TAX (from tax tables)

minus

CREDIT FOR THE ELDERLY OR DISABLED

equals

INCOME TAX DUE

Special Tax Provisions

The following types of income and expense are subject to special tax treatment. The starred (*) items are aimed specifically at senior citizens. Review those that apply to you.

CAPITAL GAINS AND LOSSES

Capital gains are profits realized from the sale of assets (such as property and investments), and capital losses are losses incurred from the sale of assets. Any profit is a capital gain, but not all losses are capital losses. For example, if you buy a car for $5,000 and sell it two years later for $3,500, you can't claim a capital loss, because automobiles are expected to decline in value through normal wear and tear. Hence, assets that are used—autos, boats, appliances—do not qualify for capital loss deductions. Beginning in 1988, capital gains are taxable at the ordinary income rate to the extent they exceed capital losses incurred during the year. If you incur capital losses, they're deductible from gross taxable income as adjustments to the extent that they exceed capital gains, but not more than $3,000 may be deducted in a single year. For example, if you had capital gains of $2,000 and capital losses of $6,000 this year, your net capital loss would be $4,000. You could deduct $3,000 this year and the remaining $1,000 next year.

401(K) PLANS

These retirement plans are available to employees of the more than 1,000 companies that sponsor them. They allow you to contribute before-tax earnings, up to a maximum set by the corporation but not to exceed $7,313 in 1988, adjusted annually for inflation. Usually, the company will match part or all of your contribution. Check with your employee benefits department to see if your company offers this plan.

403(B) PLANS

These retirement plans are available to employees of non-profit organizations such as hospitals, public schools, colleges, and universities. They allow you to contribute up to 16⅔% of your before-tax earnings (not to exceed $9,000 per year) and choose from a variety of savings and investment options. You may also make extra contributions for prior years in which you did not participate.

*GAIN ON THE SALE OF A PERSONAL RESIDENCE

You can exclude from your gross taxable income a tax-free capital gain of up to $125,000 from the sale of your personal residence if you fulfill the following qualifications: (1) You must have owned and lived in the home for at least three of the last five years. (2) You must be at least 55 years old. (3) You (or your spouse) cannot have taken this benefit before; if you marry someone who has taken the tax-free gain, you're not entitled to it, even if you weren't married when the gain was realized.

INDIVIDUAL RETIREMENT ACCOUNTS (IRAs)

If you are a wage earner under age 70½, you can enjoy the benefits of an IRA—your own savings or investment account in which earnings compound tax-free until you start withdrawing them, beginning as early as age 59½ or as late as age 70½. You may contribute an amount equal to your annual earnings, up to a maximum of $2,000, plus an additional $250 for your spouse if he or she doesn't earn enough to contribute. Your spouse must have a separate account, and you can divide your contribution between both accounts, as long as one account receives no less than $250. For example, if your spouse is several years younger and you want the funds to compound longer before you must begin withdrawal, you may contribute $2,000 to your spouse's account and $250 to yours. If you are not covered by a retirement plan (Keogh, 401(k), 403(b), or other pension plan) where you work, your contribution is considered an adjustment and reduces your gross taxable income, dollar for dollar. Even if you are covered by a company plan, if your adjusted gross income (before deducting your IRA contribution) is $40,000 or less for a married couple and $25,000 or less for a single individual, you may deduct as an adjustment the amount you contribute. If you're married and earn between $40,000 and $50,000 or single and earn between $25,000 and $35,000, your contribution is partially deductible (deductibility drops by 10% for each additional $1,000 of earnings). Withdrawals from an IRA prior to age 59½, except in the case of death or disability, will be subject to a 10% non-deductible tax penalty. You must begin withdrawing from your IRA no later than April 1st of the year following the year in which you attain the age of 70½.

*KEOGH PLANS

If you are a sole proprietor or partner or employed by a sole proprietorship or partnership, you may enjoy the benefits of a tax-sheltered Keogh plan. There are two types of Keogh plans—defined contribution and defined benefit.

The defined contribution plan allows you to contribute up to 20% of your before-tax earnings to a maximum of $30,000 annually. As the proprietor or partner, you may choose from many savings or investment options; as an employee, the contribution is made on your behalf. In either case, you can make an additional voluntary after-tax contribution: the lesser of 10% of earnings or $2,500. All contributions compound in the plan, tax-free, until withdrawn at retirement.

The defined benefit Keogh plan is advantageous to the over-50 business owner who wants to shelter maximum earnings. The annual contribution is computed actuarily and is based on a future retirement goal. The closer you are to retirement, the greater your contribution can be, with the maximum annual amount set at $90,000. If you leave the company or retire, you can transfer your Keogh account to your own IRA without tax consequence (the transfer must be accomplished within 60 days of receipt of the plan proceeds) and continue to compound your earnings, tax-free.

*SOCIAL SECURITY BENEFITS

Social Security benefits are tax-exempt unless: adjusted gross income (AGI) + municipal bond interest + 50% of Social Security benefits is greater than $25,000 for a single filer or $32,000 for a married couple filing jointly (the "base amount"). The taxable amount is the lesser of: 50% of the amount in excess of the base amount *or* 50% of the Social Security benefit. For example, Jim Smith, a single individual, had an adjusted gross income of $30,000, earned $5,000 in municipal bond interest, and received $7,000 in Social Security benefits. The amount in excess of the base amount is $13,500 ($30,000 + $5,000 + ½ of $7,000 − $25,000). Since 50% of his Social Security benefit (½ of $7,000 = $3,500) is less than 50% of the amount in excess (½ of $13,500 = $6,750), $3,500 of his Social Security benefit is taxable income.

*REPEAL OF THE THREE-YEAR RULE FOR GOVERNMENT EMPLOYEES

Beginning on July 1, 1986, employees of federal, state, and local governments cannot take advantage of a prior provision that allowed them to withdraw their own pension plan contributions within three years after retiring without incurring any tax. If you contributed all or part of the cost of your pension or annuity, part of each payment you receive is now taxable. Each payment is made up of two parts: the return of your money (the tax-free part) and your employer's contribution plus interest earned on the account (the taxable part). For example, if Ilene Harris receives a $500 monthly pension benefit, of which 20% is deemed to be her contribution, 80% of the $500 benefit ($400) is taxable income.

*INTEREST EXCLUSION FOR RECIPIENTS OF LIFE INSURANCE BENEFITS

Life insurance proceeds paid to you as beneficiary of the deceased are generally not taxable. If the insured was your spouse, and the proceeds are held by the insurance company in an interest-bearing account and paid to you in installments, $1,000 per year of the interest portion of the installment is tax-exempt. For example, Sara Wilson decides to receive the proceeds of her deceased husband's $50,000 life insurance policy in ten annual installments of $7,500. The amount of each installment that is considered non-taxable life insurance proceeds is $5,000 [the amount of the benefit ($50,000) divided by the number of installments (101)]. The remaining amount ($7,500 − $5,000 = $2,500) is considered taxable interest. Since, $1,000 of annual interest is excluded from tax, Sara's annual taxable proceeds are $1,500 ($2,500 − the $1,000 annual exclusion).

What Is Your Tax Filing Status?

Your filing status determines which Tax Rate Schedule you use to compute your tax liability. There are three basic classifications: single, married couple filing jointly, and head of household.

You must file as a *single individual* if, on the last day of the tax year, you were unmarried or divorced (or separated under a separate maintenance agreement) and do not qualify for another filing status.

You may file as a *married couple filing jointly* if you are married or if your spouse died during the tax year. You may also file separate returns, but it's likely that your tax will be higher. You may file as a *qualifying widow or widower* (and be taxed the same as a *married couple filing jointly*) if you meet all of the following requirements: (1) your spouse died during the two years prior to the tax year; (2) you did not remarry before the end of the tax year; (3) you contributed more than half the cost of the upkeep of your home, which served as the primary residence of your dependent child for the entire tax year.

You may file as a *head of household*, whose rates are lower than for a single individual, if: (1) you were unmarried on the last day of the tax year, and (2) you paid more than half the cost of the upkeep of your home that was the primary residence for: your unmarried child, your married child whom you claim as a dependent, your mother or father, and certain other relatives. Note: Your parent does not have to live with you for you to qualify for this filing status. You qualify if you provide more than half the support of your parent's household, whether it's a residence, rest home, or nursing facility.

The Tax Impact of Divorce

A divorce is painful at any stage of life, but for the older person, it can be especially traumatic. Those who've depended on a spouse for companionship may find that a shared living arrangement will help them adjust to being single. From a financial standpoint, it's vital that each spouse keep track of monthly expenses, so that an agreement as to the division of assets can be equitably reached. If alimony is granted, it's treated as taxable income to the recipient and as a tax deduction for the payer. Under the tax reform legislation, it's likely that the recipient will pay less tax on alimony than previously. If there's a division of appreciated property, the recipient will owe tax on the profit when it's sold.

The former spouse of a person who receives Social Security retirement or disability benefits is entitled to a benefit on the recipient's record if he or she is at least 62 years old (60 years old for a surviving former spouse) and they were married for at least ten years. Generally, a divorced spouse must be unmarried when applying for benefits. A divorced spouse who has been divorced at least two years can receive benefits at age 62 whether or not the former spouse receives them.

Worksheets 15 and 16: Calculating Your Taxes

To estimate your tax liability and highest (marginal) tax rate for the current year, follow the instructions for each item below. The line numbers the worksheet refers to on IRS Form 1040 are from the 1988 form, so if your income for this year will be about the same, use those numbers. The following line numbers refer to Worksheet 15. The starred (*) items are subject to special tax treatment, explained beginning on page 113.

(L1) Total your items of *gross taxable income*, which *include*:

Wages and commissions
Interest on savings accounts, money market funds, government and corporate bonds
Stock dividends
Pension benefits (excluding the amount you contributed)
Disability benefits
*Capital gains (profits realized from sales of assets)
Alimony received
Rents and royalties
Distributions (withdrawals) from IRA, Keogh, 401(k), and 403(b) plans

But *exclude*:

*Social Security benefits
Municipal bond interest
*Earnings accumulation in IRAs, Keoghs, 401(k)s, 403(b)s
Gifts and inheritances
*Life insurance proceeds (paid to beneficiary upon death of insured)

(L2) Total the following amounts, which are called *adjustments*:

*Contributions to IRA and Keogh plans
Alimony payments
*Capital losses incurred from the sale of assets (maximum $3,000/year)
Penalty charges for premature certificate of deposit withdrawals

(L3) Subtract your total adjustments (L2) from your total gross income (L1) to determine your *adjusted gross income (AGI)*.

(L4) Total your *itemized deductions*, which include:

Charitable donations
State and local income and property taxes
Unreimbursed health care costs to extent total exceeds 7.5% of AGI (L3)
Mortgage interest on a primary and secondary residence
Margin interest to the extent of dividend and interest income; then deductible to the same extent as consumer interest
Consumer interest (e.g., credit card debt, auto financing): 65% deductible in 1987; 40% deductible in 1988; 20% deductible in 1989; 10% deductible in 1990; not deductible thereafter
Unreimbursed casualty losses to extent total exceeds 10% of AGI (L3) + $100
Miscellaneous deductions (e.g., money management, accounting fees, union dues) to the extent the total exceeds 2% of AGI (L3)

(L5) Determine the amount of your *standard deduction:*
Standard Deduction for 1988
$5,000 for a married couple filing jointly
$3,000 for a single individual
$4,400 for a head of household
Plus: $600 for a married person who is elderly or blind ($1,200 if both) or $750 for a single person who is elderly or blind ($1,500 if both)

(L6) Determine the amount you can deduct from your adjusted gross income—the greater of: your itemized deductions (L4) or your standard deduction (L5).

(L7) Determine the amount of your *personal exemptions:* Multiply by number of family members: $1,900 in 1987; $1,950 in 1988; $2,000 in 1989; adjusted for inflation thereafter.

(L8) Determine the amount of your *net taxable income* by subtracting both L6 (the greater of your itemized deductions or your standard deduction) and L7 (your personal exemptions) from L3 (your adjusted gross income). This is the value that determines your tax liability.

(L9–L12) Consult the tax table on page 127 to compute your *tax liability*.

(L13) Determine whether you're entitled to a *credit for the elderly or disabled* by using Worksheet 16.

(L14) Subtract the credit (L13) from your tax liability (L12) to determine the amount of *income tax you owe*.

(L15) Consult the tax table on page 127 to determine your *marginal tax rate*.

WORKSHEET 15

What Are Your Projected Tax Liability and Tax Rate?

(L1) What is the total amount of your gross taxable income? _____
      (Line 23 on IRS Form 1040)

(L2) What is the total amount of your adjustments? _____
      (Line 30 on IRS Form 1040)

(L3) What is your adjusted gross income (AGI)? _____
      [Line 31 on IRS Form 1040 or (L1 − L2)]

(L4) What is the total amount of your itemized deductions? _____
      (Line 26 on IRS Schedule A)

(L5) What is the total amount of your standard deduction? _____
      (see page 119)

(L6) How much can you deduct from AGI? _____
      (the larger of L4 or L5)

(L7) What is the total amount of your personal exemptions? _____
      (see page 119)

(L8) What is your net taxable income? _____
      (L3 − L6 − L7)

(L9) First (lower) number in range of Column 1 (Net Taxable Income) of tax table
      on page 127 that includes L8 _____

(L10) Subtract L9 from L8 _____

(L11) Multiply L10 by Column 3 (% on Excess) of tax table _____

(L12) What is your projected tax liability? _____
       [L11 + Column 2 (Tax) of tax table]

Complete Worksheet 16 to determine whether you're entitled to a tax credit. Calculate your tax liability as follows:

(L13) What is the amount of your credit for the elderly? _____
       (L7 on Worksheet 16)

(L14) What is your projected income tax due? _____
       (L12 − L13)

(L15) What is your tax rate? _____
       Locate range in Column 1 of tax table that includes L14 and read across to
       Column 3 (% on Excess); this is your highest (marginal) tax rate.

WORKSHEET 16

Do You Qualify for the Credit for the Elderly or Disabled?

If you're age 65 or older or under age 65 and retired on permanent and total disability, you qualify for a credit to reduce your tax liability. To figure the credit, you must first determine your "base amount" (L1). If you're under 65, your base amount cannot be more than your taxable disability income for the tax year. If you're 65 or older and:

- Single, head of household, qualifying widow or widower, L1 is $5,000
- Married, filing jointly, but only one spouse qualifies, L1 is $5,000
- Married, filing jointly, and both of you qualify, L1 is $7,500
- Married, filing separately, and don't live with spouse, L1 is $3,750

(L1) What is your "base amount"? _____

(L2) How much did you receive in non-taxable Social Security benefits and pensions? _____

(L3) What is your adjusted gross income (AGI)? _____
(Line 31 on Form 1040 or L3 on Worksheet 15)

(L4) What is your "adjusted gross income limit"? _____
$7,500 if you're single, head of household, qualifying widow or widower
$10,000 if you're married and filing jointly
$5,000 if you're married, filing separately, and don't live with spouse

(L5) What is your excess adjusted gross income? _____
[(L3 − L4) divided by 2]

(L6) How much of your income qualifies for credit? _____
(L1 − L2 − L5)

(L7) How much is your credit? _____
(L6 × .15)

Sample: The Atkinses Do Their Taxes

Grace and Paul Atkins, a couple in their early 70s, neither of whom is blind, calculated their tax liability, using a combination of last year's and this year's figures.

SAMPLE WORKSHEET 15:

What Is the Atkinses' Projected Tax Liability and Tax Rate?

(L1) What is the total amount of your gross taxable income? (Line 23 on IRS Form 1040) — *12,667*

(L2) What is the total amount of your adjustments? (Line 30 on IRS Form 1040) — *500*

(L3) What is your adjusted gross income (AGI)? [Line 31 on IRS Form 1040 or (L1 − L2)] — *12,167*

(L4) What is the total amount of your itemized deductions? (Line 26 on IRS Schedule A) — *3,630*

(L5) What is the total amount of your standard deduction? (see page 119) — *6,200*

(L6) How much can you deduct from AGI? (the larger of L4 or L5) — *6,200*

(L7) What is the total amount of your personal exemptions? (see page 119) — *3,800*

(L8) What is your net taxable income? (L3 − L6 − L7) — *2,167*

(L9) First (lower) number in range of Column 1 (Net Taxable Income) of tax table on page 127 that includes L8 — *0*

(L10) Subtract L9 from L8 — *2,167*

(L11) Multiply L10 by Column 3 (% on Excess) of tax table — *325*

(L12) What is your projected tax liability? [L11 + Column 2 (Tax) of tax table] — *325*

Complete Worksheet 16 to determine whether you're entitled to a tax credit. Calculate your tax liability as follows:

(L13) What is the amount of your credit for the elderly? (L7 on Worksheet 16) — *212*

(L14) What is your projected income tax due? (L12 − L13) — *113*

(L15) What is your tax rate? Locate range in Column 1 of tax table that includes L14 and read across to Column 3 (% on Excess); this is your highest (marginal) tax rate. — *15%*

They expect their total gross taxable income (L1) to be about the same as last year ($12,667). They had no adjustments on Line 29, Form 1040, but cashed in a certificate of deposit this month and incurred a penalty charge of $500, so they entered that amount on L2. Subtracting it from gross taxable income, they arrived at their adjusted gross income (AGI)—the basis for calculating deductions for medical expenses, casualty losses, and miscellaneous expenses—of $12,167. Their total amount of itemized deductions last year was $650 and they don't expect much more this year. Paul explained, "Grace was ill this past year and we had to pay some of the expense the insurance didn't cover, but now that our medical costs have to exceed 7.5% of AGI, only $1,087 of the $2,000 we spent on insurance and medical care is deductible. Adding that to our mortgage interest expense, we could only come up with $3,630 in itemized deductions, far less than the standard deduction of $6,200 we're entitled to." The Atkinses then subtracted the standard deduction and the value of two personal exemptions in 1987 ($1,900 × 2) from their AGI to arrive at a net taxable income of $2,167.

To compute their projected tax liability for the year, they consulted the tax table on page 127 under Married Couples Filing Joint Returns. Their income falls in the Column 1 range between $0 and $29,750, so they multiplied their net taxable income ($2,167) by the "% on Excess" in Column 3 (15%) and added it to the "Tax" in Column 2 (0) to determine their tax liability—$325.

The Atkinses then filled in Worksheet 16 to find out whether they qualified for the credit for the elderly.

SAMPLE WORKSHEET 16:

Do the Atkinses Qualify for the Credit for the Elderly or Disabled?

If you're age 65 or older or under age 65 and retired on permanent and total disability, you qualify for a credit to reduce your tax liability. To figure the credit, you must first determine your "base amount" (L1). If you're under 65, your base amount cannot be more than your taxable disability income for the tax year. If you're 65 or older and:

- Single, head of household, qualifying widow or widower, L1 is $5,000
- Married, filing jointly, but only one spouse qualifies, L1 is $5,000
- Married, filing jointly, and both of you qualify, L1 is $7,500
- Married, filing separately, and don't live with spouse, L1 is $3,750

(L1) What is your "base amount"?   **7,500**

(L2) How much did you receive in non-taxable Social Security benefits and pensions?   **5,000**

(L3) What is your adjusted gross income (AGI)?   **12,167**
(Line 31 on Form 1040 or L3 on Worksheet 15)

(L4) What is your "adjusted gross income limit"?   **10,000**
$7,500 if you're single, head of household, qualifying widow or widower
$10,000 if you're married and filing jointly
$5,000 if you're married, filing separately, and don't live with spouse

(L5) What is your excess adjusted gross income?   **1,084**
[(L3 − L4) divided by 2]

(L6) How much of your income qualifies for credit?   **1,416**
(L1 − L2 − L5)

(L7) How much is your credit?   **212**
(L6 × .15)

> **Checklist: How to Maximize Your Tax Deductions**

There are two methods of reducing income taxes: *maximizing deductions* for the current year and *deferring income* to future years. If you've been able to benefit from itemized deductions previously, you'll need more of them since the tax law changed. Check the following tax savers:

_____ *Use your charge cards for deductible purchases at year end.* Expenses you charge this year can be deducted this year, even though you pay for them next year. Your statement also provides documentation for your deductions.

_____ *Postpone charitable donations to year end.* You'll know how much you can afford to give and have the use of your money all year long.

_____ *Offset capital gains with capital losses, if possible.* Losses are deductible up to a limit of $3,000 a year but are fully deductible to the extent of any capital gains you receive.

_____ *Deduct the cost of worthless securities and bad debts.* If you own a stock or bond of a company that's gone out of business, you must deduct your cost in the year the security becomes worthless. The same is true of bad debts.

_____ *Plan elective medical and dental care at year end.* If it's covered by insurance, you can still deduct the full expense of eyeglasses, hearing aids, dental work, or surgery in the current year and report your insurance reimbursement as taxable income next year, when you receive it.

_____ *Deduct this year's disaster loss last year.* If you sustain a casualty loss in a location that the President has designated a disaster area, you can claim the loss in either the current or the preceding year. By taking the deduction last year, you get an immediate refund.

_____ *Bunch deductions in alternate years.* If it doesn't pay for you to itemize, try to shift deductible expenses so that you have a lot one year and a little the next. For example, pay two years' property taxes in one year, and then skip the next.

————— *Keep records of medical expenses.* Many small bills can add up to a deductible amount. To document your expenses, be certain to keep receipts for dentures, hearing aid batteries, prescription medications, insulin and syringes. You can also deduct the cost of transportation to and from the doctor's office (9 cents per mile if you don't use public transportation) and parking fees.

————— *Postpone year-end receipt of taxable income to January 2nd.* By waiting a few days, you postpone taxes on the income for a whole year

————— *Invest in securities that mature next year.* After July 1st, put some of your savings in six-month certificates of deposit or U.S. Treasury Bills that pay interest when they mature, after the first of the year.

Federal Income Tax Tables for 1988

Column 1 Net Taxable Income	Column 2 Tax	Column 3 % on Excess
MARRIED COUPLES FILING JOINT RETURNS		
$ 0– 29,750	$ 0	15%
29,751– 71,900	4,463	28%
71,901–149,250	16,265	33%
149,251 and over	41,790	28%*
SINGLE INDIVIDUALS		
$ 0–17,850	$ 0	15%
17,851–43,150	2,678	28%
43,151–89,560	9,762	33%
89,561 and over	25,077	28%*
HEADS OF HOUSEHOLD		
$ 0– 23,900	$ 0	15%
23,901– 61,650	3,585	28%
61,651–123,790	14,155	33%
123,791 and over	34,661	28%*

* Plus a surcharge of 5% on income over $149,250 ($89,560 for a single individual and $123,790 for heads of household) to a maximum of $546 × the number of personal exemptions. Example: A family of four (four exemptions) would pay the surcharge ($2,184) on the next $43,680 of income. Income over $192,930 would be taxed at 28%.

Protecting Yourself From Economic Uncertainty

OBJECTIVE: To put your money to work effectively. Where can you get the best return on your savings, with minimum risk? Should you invest in stocks, bonds, or other vehicles? If so, which are the right ones and how much should you invest? Are you the owner or beneficiary of a life insurance policy? Would you like it to pay you a monthly income for as long as you live? How should you withdraw your pension plan or IRA?

WHAT YOU WILL NEED

Bank, savings and loan, and securities statements

Today's economic environment is fraught with uncertainty. Interest rates, stock prices, and property values are in a constant state of flux. Hardly a day goes by that you don't read about some new investment that's designed to protect you from the hazards that all the others possess. It's difficult to resist the feeling that, if you could predict the direction of the economy, you could profit from its gyrations. Yet the more volatile it becomes, the riskier it is to try to outguess it. What can you do to preserve the value of your savings and make certain that they're working as hard for you as they should? Let the following six "don'ts" be your guide.

Six Steps to Smart Saving

1. DON'T put your money into anything that causes you worry. If you feel uneasy about it, if it keeps you awake at night, if you find yourself thinking about it frequently, then it's not for you. Put your money only in those vehicles that you feel comfortable and secure with.

2. DON'T put your money into anything you don't fully understand. Before you write a check, ask these questions: How much of my money goes to work for me? What can go wrong? How can I get my money out? If I needed to get my money back, what would I stand to lose? What guarantee do I have that the investment will perform as promised? Request printed literature to back up any promises made by brokers or salespeople.

3. DON'T buy from dealers who are unfamiliar to you. Older people are the favorite prey of high-pressure telephone sales operations that sell land, precious metals, and other high-risk commodities. Even if you're lucky enough to make money, smooth-talking sales representatives will convince you to reinvest in another "special situation"—and you won't be rid of them until they're certain your capital is gone. If someone tries to sell you something over the phone and you can't convince them that you want to think about it, just hang up.

4. DON'T buy what everybody's buying. Market cycles are caused by supply and demand. When everybody wants something, the price goes up—until there are no more buyers. When it seems as though prices will continue to rise forever, then the smart sellers will begin taking profits and drive prices down. Don't be the last buyer—try to be among the first to buy what's likely to be popular next.

5. DON'T buy what your friends are buying. Just as taking someone else's medication can be disastrous, so can taking their investment advice. People tend to brag about their successes and often neglect to tell you about their failures. Select what's right for you.

6. DON'T move your money around frequently. Trying to predict market turns is an exercise in futility and will only wind up costing you money. Market timing services and prognosticators base their predictions on historical precedent. History may repeat itself, but never in precisely the same way. Put your money in sound vehicles and leave it there to grow and compound.

Selecting the Best Savings Vehicle(s)

There are two ways of making your capital work for you: you can put it into either a savings vehicle or an investment vehicle. A savings vehicle is one in which there is little or no risk of losing the money you deposit—you can withdraw your principal tomorrow, six months, or six years from now and be assured that it will remain intact. Savings vehicles include checking, passbook, and money market accounts, and money market funds. These are sometimes referred to as cash equivalents or liquid accounts because money can flow in or out without the threat of loss or penalty. To make the best use of a savings vehicle, follow these guidelines:

1. Keep only as much money in a non-interest-bearing account (checking account) as you need to cover one month's expenses. The rest of your money should be earning interest for you.

2. Find out whether your account is insured. Bank and savings and loan accounts are insured by agencies of the federal government: the Federal Deposit Insurance Corporation (FDIC) covers banks, and the Federal Savings & Loan Insurance Corporation (FSLIC) insures savings and loan associations for up to $100,000 per insured account. If you have a checking account, savings account, and certificates of deposit all registered in your name alone, they are considered one insured account and the total value is insured for up to $100,000. If you have a joint account with a spouse, an IRA account, and an individual account, they are considered three separate insured accounts and the total value is insured for up to $300,000. If you have joint accounts with your spouse and each of your children, half of the total value is considered one insured account and is insured for up to $100,000. Don't allow the amount in your accounts to exceed the insurance limitations at any one bank. Open an account in another financial institution, if necessary.

3. Select accounts that are right for you. The various types of accounts are designed to meet different needs. There's no sense in earning less interest or paying charges on an account in exchange for services you don't need or use.

How much of your money should you have in a savings vehicle? *Up to 100% of it!* Some so-called experts may try to convince you that you have to put your money into an investment—such as stocks, real estate, and gold—in order to keep up with inflation and to be certain of financial security. This just isn't so. Money market rates are directly tied to inflation rates, so that if the rate of inflation rises, so will the return on your savings vehicle. As the graph below illustrates, this has been true as far back as 1960.

While an investment offers you the potential for a higher return, it also entails a greater degree of risk. The value of a savings vehicle will increase steadily because it's always earning some rate of compounded return, but an investment may be worth more—or less—than what you paid for it at any point in the future:

	Less	**Starting Amount**	**More**
Savings vehicle		$100	⟶
Investment vehicle	⟵	$100	⟶

This difference is especially important to the older person, who may not live to see an investment bear fruit. Investment vehicles are attractive because they offer the potential for a much greater return than one could receive from a savings vehicle, but it may be many years before that return is realized. The highest annual return one can hope to earn on savings, historically speaking, is 15% or 16% (money market funds paid this rate during 1980). Investments, on the other hand, can produce compounded annual returns of 20% or more.

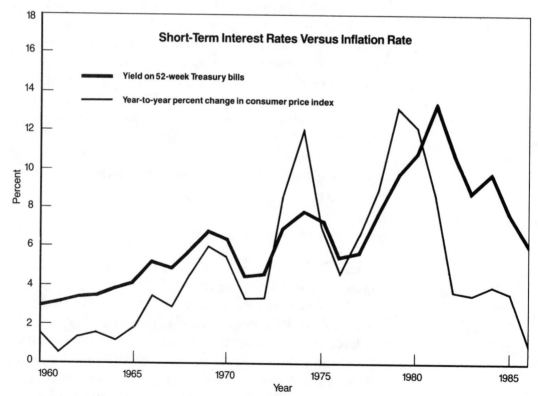

Sources: U.S. Department of Labor Bureau of Labor Statistics and Federal Reserve System.

Money Market Funds

FEATURES

Money market funds are sponsored by investment companies and brokerage firms. Deposits are handled by mail and you receive a monthly statement of earnings and account activity. The minimum deposit required to open an account is usually $500 to $1,000, and most require additions of a minimum amount, usually $50 or more. You receive a checkbook, which allows you to write unlimited checks at no charge; however, checks must be written for a minimum of $250 or more. Your money is invested in very short-term government and corporate securities and you purchase "shares" in the fund, with each share having a stable (unchanging) value of $1. If you deposit $1,000, you will purchase 1,000 shares. These accounts are not insured but are considered safe because of the safety and short duration of secu-

TAX-FREE VERSUS TAXABLE INCOME—WHICH IS BETTER FOR YOU?

Tax-exempt money market funds, bonds, and unit trusts usually pay a lower rate of interest than comparable taxable securities, but if your tax rate is 28% or more, they may pay you a higher after-tax return.

To determine what a taxable security would have to yield to equal the yield of a tax-free security (or vice versa), locate your net taxable income or tax rate in the left-hand columns of the following table and read across.

A TAX-FREE YIELD OF

1988 Taxable Income	Tax Rate	4.5%	5%	5.5%	6%	6.5%	7%	7.5%	8%	8.5%	9%	9.5%	10%
		IS EQUIVALENT TO A TAXABLE YIELD OF											
Single Individuals													
$0–$17,850	15%	5.3%	5.9%	6.5%	7%	7.6%	8.2%	8.8%	9.4%	10%	10.6%	11.2%	11.8%
$17,851–$43,150	28%	6.3%	6.9%	7.6%	8.3%	9%	9.7%	10.4%	11.1%	11.8%	12.5%	13.2%	13.9%
$43,151–$89,560	33%	6.7%	7.5%	8.2%	9%	9.7%	10.4%	11.2%	11.9%	12.7%	13.4%	14.2%	14.9%
$89,561 and over	28%	6.3%	6.9%	7.6%	8.3%	9%	9.7%	10.4%	11.1%	11.8%	12.5%	13.2%	13.9%
Married Couples Filing Joint Returns													
$0–$29,750	15%	5.3%	5.9%	6.5%	7%	7.6%	8.2%	8.8%	9.4%	10%	10.6%	11.2%	11.8%
$29,751–$71,900	28%	6.3%	6.9%	7.6%	8.3%	9%	9.7%	10.4%	11.1%	11.8%	12.5%	13.2%	13.9%
$71,901–$149,250	33%	6.7%	7.5%	8.2%	9%	9.7%	10.4%	11.2%	11.9%	12.7%	13.4%	14.2%	14.9%
$149,251 and over	28%	6.3%	6.9%	7.6%	8.3%	9%	9.7%	10.4%	11.1%	11.8%	12.5%	13.2%	13.9%
Heads of Household													
$0–$23,900	15%	5.3%	5.9%	6.5%	7%	7.6%	8.2%	8.8%	9.4%	10%	10.6%	11.2%	11.8%
$23,901–$61,650	28%	6.3%	6.9%	7.6%	8.3%	9%	9.7%	10.4%	11.1%	11.8%	12.5%	13.2%	13.9%
$61,651–$123,790	33%	6.7%	7.5%	8.2%	9%	9.7%	10.4%	11.2%	11.9%	12.7%	13.4%	14.2%	14.9%
$123,791 and over	28%	6.3%	6.9%	7.6%	8.3%	9%	9.7%	10.4%	11.1%	11.8%	12.5%	13.2%	13.9%

rities. The yield changes with current market conditions and is often slightly higher than that of money market accounts sponsored by banks and savings and loans. Tax-exempt money market funds are invested in very short-term tax-exempt securities of states and municipalities. These pay a lower yield but may be more advantageous for you if you're in the highest tax bracket.

ADVANTAGES

These usually pay a slightly higher return than other savings vehicles.

DISADVANTAGES

Because of the check-writing minimum, you can't use these accounts for all of your checking needs. You aren't dealing with a local institution (brokerage firms prefer not to handle deposits and withdrawals unless you're an active securities client); and some merchants will not accept out-of-state checks. If lack of insurance is a concern, only those funds that invest solely in U.S. government securities should be considered.

Asset Management Accounts

FEATURES

These all-in-one accounts are sponsored by major banks and brokerage firms. They combine many features, including a money market fund, checking account, securities account, and a charge card (may be optional). Deposits are handled by mail and you receive a monthly statement of earnings and account activity. Minimum deposit to open an account is $10,000 to $20,000 in cash and/or securities. Additions are usually required to be a minimum of $50 or more. You receive a checkbook which allows you to write an unlimited number of checks in any amount, so that this account can be used for most of your check-writing needs. Interest or dividends earned on securities are automatically added to your money market fund (you may choose between a regular, government, or tax-free money fund). Your charge card purchases (MasterCard, Visa, or American Express) are deducted either at the time the charge is posted to the account or at the end of the month. The annual fee ranges from about $30 to $150, depending upon the services you use.

ADVANTAGES

You may find it convenient to have your investments and savings all in one place, with dividend and interest checks automatically deposited (daily or weekly) in your money market fund. Some investment firms and banks offer discount brokerage service—the transaction amount is added to or deducted from your account on the appropriate date, and you can use the account for most checking needs. Aggregate securities in the account are insured by the Securities Investors Protection Corporation (SIPC) for at least $500,000 and credit balances are insured for up to $100,000. SIPC is a government agency that protects assets held by brokerage firms from losses caused by a firm's failure. It does not, however, protect investors from a decline in the value of their investments due to market conditions.

DISADVANTAGES

There is a high minimum to open an account. Out-of-town checks may not be accepted by local merchants. There are annual fees. Debit card charges are deducted when posted to the account.

Bank and Savings and Loan Accounts

FEATURES

Since 1986, when interest rate ceilings on savings deposits were completely phased out, commercial banks, mutual savings banks, and savings and loan associations have spawned many types of accounts. The most popular are the traditional passbook savings account, NOW (negotiated order of withdrawal), and money market accounts. Generally speaking, the higher the yield on the account, the greater the number of restrictions. However, many financial institutions waive fees and restrictions for senior citizens. Money market accounts pay a rate of interest that's pegged to current interest rates, require that you maintain a minimum balance (usually $2,500), and limit you to three free checks a month. Passbook savings accounts often have no minimum deposit and also pay a rate of interest that is tied to current rates. Each separate account is insured by a government agency for up to $100,000. Bank accounts are insured by the Federal Deposit Insurance Corporation (FDIC) and savings and loan accounts by the Federal Savings and Loan Association Corporation (FSLIC).

ADVANTAGES

These are considered to be the safest of the savings vehicles because they're federally insured. You can access cash quickly by withdrawing funds or cashing a check. Banks and savings and loans provide other services you may require, such as safe deposit boxes, short- and long-term loans, and traveler's checks.

DISADVANTAGES

Many financial institutions impose charges if your account drops below a certain balance or if you write more than the allowed number of checks a month. The rate paid on a money market account is usually slightly lower than you'd earn on a money market fund.

WORKSHEET 17
Select the Best Savings Vehicles

1. Do you want maximum safety? YES NO

If you desire maximum safety, choose a *bank or savings account* in an institution that's protected by federal insurance. The yield may be ¼% to ½% lower than that paid by a money market fund, but this is not significant enough to warrant sleepless nights.

2. Do you write many checks? YES NO

Both a *central assets account* and a non-interest-bearing *checking account* permit unlimited free check-writing. If you choose the checking account, maintain only the minimum balance required to avoid charges plus the average amount of your monthly checks. Replenish the account monthly from your interest-bearing account.

3. Do you own stocks or bonds? YES NO

A *central assets account* automatically deposits your stock dividends and bond interest checks in your money market fund. Your money goes to work more quickly than if you received checks directly and had to mail in deposits yourself. Your securities are insured for a minimum of $500,000 and you can sell them immediately, if the need arises, and avoid the delay of removing them from a safe deposit box and transporting them to a brokerage firm.

4. Do you want a higher yield? YES NO

A *money market fund* will pay you the highest yield available on a savings vehicle.

5. Do you desire local convenience? YES NO

Many people who've experienced the Depression don't feel comfortable mailing their money out of state. If you prefer to have your money where you live, a *local bank or savings and loan* is best for you.

6. Are you in a high tax bracket? YES NO

If your income level puts you in the highest tax bracket, you may be able to earn a higher after-tax return in a *tax-exempt money market fund.* Check the chart on page 133 to compare taxable and tax-free yields. Caveat: A tax-exempt money market fund maintains a stable share value and is not the same as a tax-exempt bond fund, which invests in bonds and fluctuates in value.

7. Do you have a small account (less than $500)?   YES   NO

In order to avoid costly charges and fees, you may be best served by a *passbook savings account* that requires no minimum balance.

8. Are you willing to maintain more than one account?   YES   NO

A combination of accounts may serve your needs best. For example, a money market fund plus a local checking account provide local convenience and a place to obtain cash quickly and deposit small checks along with a savings vehicle that will produce a higher return.

Evaluate your responses to this worksheet to help you determine the choice or choices that are best for you.

Selecting the Best Investment Vehicles

An investment vehicle is one in which the value of your principal—the amount you invest—is likely to change from one point in time to another. Investments include stocks, bonds, gold, collectibles, and real property. A business or enterprise you own is also considered an investment. Investments can be classified the same way you grouped your assets on your statement of net worth (Worksheet 1). For example, you can invest in a piece of property in two ways: purchase the property directly and become its owner, or lend the purchaser money to buy the property and become the mortgage holder. In the first instance, as an owner, you are responsible for maintaining and improving the property, in exchange for which you receive tax benefits, rental income, and hope to make a profit in the future, when the property is sold. In the second instance, as a lender, you have no responsibility for maintaining the property nor do you enjoy any tax benefits or appreciation potential. You do, however, receive a steady stream of income in the form of mortgage payments. Ownership entails greater risk along with the possibility of greater return. Lending your money is less risky, but your return is also likely to be less.

Whether you're an owner or a lender, your money is at risk, because there is never any certainty as to which scenario will be played out. You can minimize this risk by: (1) investing in loaned vehicles that guarantee payment of a certain rate of interest and repayment of principal at maturity; and (2) investing in vehicles that reduce your risk by spreading it over many different investments. If one should decline in value or default on interest payments, only a small portion of your capital will be lost. The following are suitable:

Guaranteed Investments	Diversified (Pooled) Investments
Series EE U.S. Savings Bonds	Mutual funds
U.S. Treasury bills, notes, & bonds	Unit trusts
Government National Mortgage Association certificates (GNMAs)	
Certificates of deposit issued by federally insured institutions	
Insured municipal bonds	
Deferred annuities from top-rated insurance companies (those rated A or A + by A. M. Best & Company, an independent evaluator of insurance companies)	

Before you invest, it's important that you recognize exactly what risks you're taking. Guaranteed investments are likely to pay you a higher rate of interest than you'd receive from a savings vehicle such as a money market fund, BUT you may not be able to withdraw all of

---

SHOULD YOU AN OWNER OR A LENDER BE?

	Owner	Lender
	COMPANY OR ENTERPRISE	
YOU GET:	Shares of stock	Bonds or notes
	The Best That Can Happen: the Company Is Successful	
RESULT:	Stock price goes up	Regular interest payments
	Dividend payments increase regularly	Repayment of principal when bond or note matures
	The Worst That Can Happen: the Company Goes Out of Business	
RESULT:	Stock price goes down	Interest payments stop
	Dividend payments stop	Bonds decline in value or become worthless
	What Is Most Likely to Happen: the Company's Profits Will Rise and Fall	
RESULT:	Stock price goes up and down	Regular interest payments
	Dividends stay the same or are increased	Repayment of principal when bond or note matures
	PROPERTY	
YOU GET:	Deed to property	Mortgage
	The Best That Can Happen: Neighborhood Becomes More Desirable	
RESULT:	Value of property goes up	Monthly repayment of interest and principal
	Rental payments increase regularly	
	The Worst That Can Happen: Neighborhood Becomes Undesirable	
RESULT:	Value of property goes down	Default on mortgage
	No one wants to rent property	Foreclosure expenses
	Maintenance costs continue	Ultimate responsibility for property
	What Is Most Likely to Happen: Continued Inflation Will Increase Value	
RESULT:	Value of property rises gradually	Monthly repayment of interest and principal
	Rental payments rise gradually	
	Maintenance costs rise gradually	

your money if you need it. Note that they guarantee repayment of principal at maturity, but what if you want your money before then? If you invest in a certificate of deposit, you'll probably have to pay a penalty charge. With a U.S. Treasury bond, the amount you receive will depend upon current interest rates. When the Federal Reserve Bank raises or lowers the discount rate (the interest rate it charges its member banks), the prices of outstanding loaned securities (IOUs)—notes, bonds, debentures, mortgages—change to adjust to this new environment. If the discount rate is increased, prices of IOUs will fall; if the rate is decreased, prices will rise. Like a see-saw, the farther out the maturity date, the greater the impact of the change. At maturity date, the value of the bond will be $1,000.

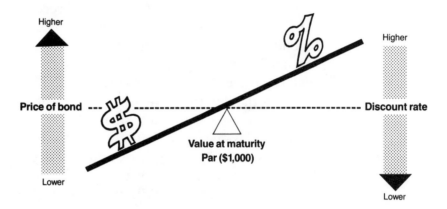

Imagine a see-saw, with interest rates on one side and bond prices on the other. Declining interest rates push the see-saw down on one side, forcing bond prices to go up on the other. The farther out your bond sits on the see-saw (the greater the time period until the bond matures), the greater the price change. Only at maturity can you be certain of getting back all of your capital.

What Happens If a Company Gets Into Financial Trouble?

If a company suffers financial reverses—from, say, increased competition, rising costs of labor and materials, mismanagement, reduced demand for the company's product or service—the company must stem its losses in order to continue to stay in business. The company is likely to invoke cost-cutting measures and try to stimulate business by diversifying its product or service line, acquiring other companies, or divesting itself of unprofitable operations. If these efforts are unsuccessful, it will be forced to:

First—Reduce the dividend paid to common stockholders
Second—Eliminate the dividend paid to common stockholders
Third—Eliminate the dividend paid to preferred stockholders
Fourth—Go bankrupt, in which case bond interest payments will cease

---

The Three "Ds" of Investment Success

1. *Derive pleasure from investing.* If you enjoy spending your leisure time researching stock and other investments, your mind will stay alert and active and you'll enhance your profit potential. The expected return on an investment is directly related to the knowledge and degree of control of the investor. A real estate investor who spends most of the day studying properties and comparing values will earn a far greater profit than someone who invests in properties without any prior knowledge or research. Similarly, a businessperson who devotes the day to actively running his or her company will do better than someone who buys a share of a business but exerts no control over its day-to-day operations. "Professional investors" invest more than just money—they invest time and energy. They are therefore entitled to receive a higher return than that paid on a savings account or money market fund. With investments, as with everything else, you get out what you put in.

2. *Demand a return.* Because all investments entail risk, and because you can't afford to wait twenty years for your investment to appreciate, do not consider any investment unless it pays interest, dividends, or current income while you wait for it to appreciate in value. Dividend-paying stocks, interest-paying mortgages and bonds, and income-producing real estate are acceptable. Tangible assets such as gold and silver, and high-risk speculations such as options and commodities, are not. If you lose money on an investment, you also lose the interest that could have been earned on the money lost. Just as savings compound, so do losses. If you're considering investing in stocks, inquire about membership in the National Association of Investment Clubs (NAIC, P.O. Box 220, Royal Oak, MI 48068), a nonprofit organization that provides investment education and publishes a monthly magazine, *Better Investing*. They also sponsor a low-cost stock investment plan and can help you organize or join an investment club in your community.

3.   *Diversify.* Don't put more than 25% of your investment capital in any one thing. Rather, spread your money among different types of investments. Diversification is even more important when you consider riskier investments. Putting a little money into a lot of risky vehicles is safer than putting a lot of money into one risky vehicle. The graph below illustrates the relative safety of various investment vehicles. Consider how much risk you are willing to take to achieve the desired return.

Most

R
E
T
U
R
N

Real estate
Common stocks
Preferred stocks
Corporate bonds *
Municipal bonds *
Annuities
Certificates of deposit
Other U.S. Government securities *
U.S. Treasury bills *

Least ──────────────────────────────────→ Most

RISK

* Because prices are affected by changing interest rates, there's no guarantee of receiving the amount you invested if sold prior to maturity. Only at maturity is return of your investment capital guaranteed.

How to Create a Diversified Investment Portfolio With Less Than $10,000

Some investments, such as U.S. Treasury notes, require a minimum purchase of $5,000. Others, such as common stocks, charge imposing fees for small purchases. How can the individual with only a few hundred to a few thousand dollars available for investment enjoy the same profit potential as the affluent person? By utilizing a mutual fund.

What is it? A mutual fund is a professionally managed portfolio of savings or investment vehicles. Money market mutual funds buy very short-term (mature in days or weeks) loaned securities. Funds also purchase a wide variety of investment vehicles, including state and U.S. government notes and bonds, GNMAs, corporate bonds, convertible securities, real estate, and common and preferred stock. Many funds specialize in a certain type of stock—those that pay high dividends or represent a certain industry, for example.

Who is it for? The mutual fund provides investment expertise, diversification, and low minimum purchase requirements (as little as $1 in some cases, but more often $500 to $1,000). It's an attractive alternative for individuals who don't feel comfortable about making specific investment decisions and/or those who have a relatively small amount of capital to invest.

How much does it cost? There are three types of fees associated with mutual funds: management fees (which are charged by all funds), sales (or load) charges, and administrative fees. The management fee pays for the ongoing management and selection of securities and ranges from about ½% to 2% of the fund's assets. If you buy shares of a fund through an intermediary, such as a stockbroker or financial planner, he or she collects from 5% to 9% of your initial investment as a sales charge, or front-end load. This one-time charge compensates your advisor for helping you select a fund that suits your needs. Sometimes the sales charge is deducted from your proceeds when you liquidate shares, in which case it's called a back-end or rear-end load. Some funds that are purchased directly through the fund sponsor may also impose a 2% to 3% (low load) sales charge. Administrative fees, sometimes referred to as "12b-1 plans," reduce your annual return by 0.25% to 1.5% to pay for advertising, printing, and distribution expenses. You're likely to earn a higher return by investing in no-load funds—those that impose low management fees and have no sales charges or 12b-1 plans.

The fund is required by law to provide you with a prospectus—a booklet that describes the fund's investments and business policies—but, unfortunately, it doesn't always reveal complete information about fees. Most funds have toll-free telephone numbers or will accept collect calls, so you can call to inquire about charges. Ask your advisor or the fund sponsor these five questions:

1. What percentage is the annual management fee?

2. What percentage of my money will be spent on sales charges?

3. Are there any withdrawal charges for redeeming shares?

4. Do you have a 12b-1 plan?

5. If so, what percentage will be withdrawn each year?

Where can you find out more about mutual funds? The most comprehensive summary of mutual fund information is the *Wiesenberger Investment Companies Service*, which is published yearly and can be found in the reference section of most public libraries. Other good resources include: *Investor's Guide and Mutual Fund Directory,* available for $5 from: No-Load Mutual Fund Association, Dept. USHC, 11 Penn Plaza, Suite 2204, New York, NY 10001, and *The Guide to Mutual Funds*, available for $1 from: The Investment Company Institute, 1600 M Street NW, Suite 600, Washington, DC 20036. The following magazines also rank mutual fund performance at least once a year: *Business Week*, *Consumer Reports*, *Forbes*, and *Money* (check your library's magazine file).

Types of No-Load Funds That Suit the Needs of the Senior Citizen

Taxable bond and mortgage mutual funds invest your money in government and corporate bonds and notes and government-backed mortgages such as GNMAs, and all pay interest that is taxable. The safest funds are those that invest only in U.S. government securities. You can increase your yield by staggering maturities. Invest part of your capital in a short-term bond fund (securities in portfolio that mature in less than three years), part in an intermediate term fund (securities that mature in three to ten years), and part in a long-term fund (more than ten-year maturities).

Tax-exempt bond funds invest in state and municipal notes and bonds and pay interest that's exempt from federal income tax. You should purchase these only if your after-tax yield is higher than that of a taxable bond fund (see page 133).

The safest bond funds are those that purchase only insured bonds.

Dividend-paying stock funds invest in stocks of large, well-established companies. Purchase those that have paid dividends in excess of 5% annually and have produced at least a 10% average annual return for the last ten years.

Real estate investment trusts (REITs) are similar to mutual funds, but they invest in real estate and mortgages. They trade like corporations on the New York Stock Exchange and you must make your initial purchase through a stockbroker or financial planner. Once you're a shareholder, you can avoid sales charges on subsequent purchases by participating in the REIT's dividend reinvestment plan. Information is mailed to you by the REIT shortly after you invest. You can obtain information on each REIT's investment policies by consulting *Value Line Investment Service* and *Standard & Poor's Stock Reports*, both available at public libraries.

Gold mutual funds invest in shares of gold mining companies. They pay dividends and—if the price of gold rises—can be expected to increase in value. These are suitable for up to 5% of your investment capital if the majority of your investment profile choices (Worksheet 19 on page 155) fall in the "Safe" category.

WORKSHEET 18

Select the Best Investments

If you have capital to invest and you want to select sound investments, this worksheet will help you determine which are best for you. Before you invest your money, be certain that you understand the risks.

1.   Do you want your investment to keep pace with inflation?   YES   NO

Real estate and commodities, such as gold, tend to increase in value during inflationary periods, and many large companies raise their dividends annually. You can spread your risk through diversification as well as earn a current return in the form of dividends by investing in REITs (real estate investment trusts) and mutual funds that specialize in dividend-paying stocks and shares of gold mining companies.

2.   Do you want to avoid transaction costs?   YES   NO

You can put all of your money to work by investing in certificates of deposit, Series EE U.S. Savings Bonds, U.S. Treasury securities (when purchased directly through a Federal Reserve bank), and no-load mutual funds.

3.   Do you want to be certain of getting a fair price should you need to sell?   YES   NO

Whenever you make an investment, it's wise to ask, "How much money could I expect to get if I were selling this investment today, rather than buying it?" Actively traded stocks of major companies (such as IBM and General Motors) have a narrower spread (the difference between what you'd pay as a buyer and what you'd receive as a seller at any point in time) than infrequently traded stocks of smaller companies. The less actively traded an investment is, the greater the spread. If there's a possibility that you might need to sell an investment early, consider U.S. Treasury securities, actively traded New York Stock Exchange stocks, or no-load mutual funds (except those that impose withdrawal fees). Avoid limited partnerships, preferred stocks, mutual funds with load charges, and unit trusts.

4.   Do you want to avoid premature withdrawal penalties?   YES   NO

Some investments impose a penalty charge if you withdraw your money within a certain time period. Purchase five $1,000 CDs rather than one $5,000 CD if there's a possibility that you'll need part of the money before maturity. Then you'll only pay the penalty on the amount you need to withdraw, rather than being penalized for cashing in the whole amount. Consider, also, staggering maturities (one CD due in one year, one in two years, etc.) so that money will regularly become available. Avoid Series EE U.S. Savings Bonds if you might need the money within five years.

5. Are you concerned about interest rates heading upward? YES NO

If interest rates rise, prices of outstanding bonds will fall because their rates will no longer be as attractive. The more distant the maturity date of the bond, the greater the impact of changing interest rates. For example, if you pay $1,000 for a bond yielding 9% and maturing in ten years, and want to sell the bond two years from now when eight-year bonds are yielding 12%, you may be able to get only $800. Even U.S. Treasury bonds guarantee return of your $1,000 only at maturity, and their values will rise and fall with changes in interest rates between now and the maturity date. If you don't want your investments to decline in value sharply because of higher rates, invest in bonds or notes that mature in three years or less. Avoid longer term bonds, mortgages, and GNMAs.

6. Do you want to receive a steady, even stream of income for several years? YES NO

Corporate and municipal bonds may appear to offer a long-term, stable return, but a period of lower interest rates may prompt the issuers of the bonds to redeem them before they mature, leaving you with cash that must be reinvested at lower rates. The same is true of mortgages and GNMAs. When interest rates drop, property owners refinance their mortgages and mortgage holders get their principal back. Consider U.S. Treasury bonds, which are the only securities that cannot be called in early (with the exception of a few that are callable five years prior to maturity), or annuity contracts, which can be structured to pay you (and your spouse) an income you can't outlive.

7. Do you desire the highest possible current return? YES NO

Risk and return go hand in hand. If you require a higher yield, you must assume a greater risk. Preferred stocks and lower quality corporate and municipal bonds pay a higher return than common stocks and top quality bonds. You can reduce this risk somewhat by investing in a mutual fund or unit trust that pools many investors' funds in order to purchase a diversified portfolio of securities.

8. Do you want investments that offer tax benefits? YES NO

If your income level elevates you to the highest tax bracket, compare taxable and tax-free yields. Consider investments that pay tax-free income, provide tax deductions, or defer income until a future time when your bracket may be lower. Municipal bonds pay a return that is federally tax-exempt (however, receipt of municipal bond income may result in taxation of your Social Security benefits—see page 116); the tax on Series EE U.S. Savings Bonds' accrued interest can be deferred until the bond is cashed in; life insurance cash value and annuity contracts defer taxes until earnings are withdrawn.

9. Do you want an income that increases over time? YES NO

Common stocks of large companies (particularly utility companies) tend to increase their dividends regularly, which rewards investors by keeping pace with inflation. Bonds, notes, certificates of deposit, and preferred stocks pay a fixed return that will not increase if inflation picks up.

10. Do you want a monthly income?   YES   NO

    If a monthly income is helpful to you in managing your budgetary needs, you should consider investments such as certificates of deposit, unit trusts, and mutual funds, all of which will send you a check each month, if you request it. Mutual funds will even allow you to specify the amount you want. However, if the value of the fund declines (due to a decline in the value of the fund's securities), some of your shares will be sold in order to maintain your desired level of income.

11. Do you want to be able to keep tabs on the value of your investment?   YES   NO

    You can check the prices of the following investments in the financial section of your daily newspaper: common stocks, mutual funds, U.S. Treasury securities, some preferred stocks, and corporate bonds.

12. Do you have only a small amount of capital available for investment?   YES   NO

    If you plan to invest less than $10,000, choose only guaranteed (certificates of deposit, Series EE U.S. Savings Bonds, and annuities) or diversified (mutual funds and unit trusts) investments. Avoid individual stock, bond, or property investments.

    Consult Appendix A (beginning on page 179) for additional information about investment vehicles, including information on where to buy, price stability, tax status, minimum amount of purchase, and transaction costs.

How Should You Withdraw Your Pension or IRA Plan?

If you participate in a company pension plan that offers you a choice of withdrawing the proceeds in a lump sum or rolling your money over into an Individual Retirement Account, your decision depends on whether or not you need the money. If you need the money now or within a few years, withdraw it and pay the taxes. Fortunately, the tax will be reduced by a special provision—called ten-year forward averaging—that applies to lump-sum pension plan withdrawals for those who attained the age of 50 on or before January 1, 1986. The tax is calculated on one-tenth of the lump sum, with minor adjustments, and then multiplied by five. If you don't need the money immediately, you'll probably come out better if you roll it over into an IRA, which must be accomplished within sixty days of receipt of funds, so that it can continue to compound tax-deferred. You'll preserve your right to withdraw funds when needed, but the amount you withdraw will be fully taxable.

How should you invest your IRA? The following investments are suitable for an IRA plan: certificates of deposit, money market funds and accounts, corporate and government bond funds, GNMA funds, and dividend-paying stock funds. Do not invest your IRA money in tax-sheltered vehicles such as municipal bonds, limited partnerships, or tax-deferred annuities. The IRA is the best tax shelter of all.

When should you begin withdrawals? Once you're 59½, you may withdraw money whenever you desire. It's best to make withdrawals in years when your taxes are likely to be low, so your withdrawals will be taxed at a lower rate. If you don't need the money, keep your IRA intact until the April 15th following the year you turn 70½. Then you must begin making withdrawals and paying tax in the year of withdrawal or face an IRS penalty of 50% of the minimum withdrawal requirement.

What is the minimum amount you can withdraw when you're 70½? If you want to keep your IRA intact for as long as possible, you can base your withdrawals on the combined life expectancies of you and your beneficiary. Assuming a joint life expectancy of, say, twenty years, you must withdraw one-twentieth of the account balance the first year. Each year, you may recompute your life expectancy and readjust the withdrawal amount. (If your beneficiary is not your spouse, the maximum age difference allowable for computing your combined life expectancy is ten years.)

What is the maximum you should withdraw? If your pension plan is worth several hundred thousand dollars or more, you could be penalized for a large withdrawal in a single year. The 1986 Tax Reform Act imposes a 15% non-deductible tax penalty on annual pension benefits that exceed $112,500.

How to Have a Steady Income for As Long As You Live

Does the prospect of receiving a steady monthly income for the rest of your life sound appealing to you? If so, perhaps you should consider investing part of your capital, the cash value or proceeds of a life insurance policy, or the proceeds from your company pension or IRA, in an annuity. Annuities are sponsored by insurance companies and are designed primarily for retired individuals and couples who desire a monthly income they can't outlive. If you want your monthly checks to begin right away, you can purchase an immediate annuity. More popular, though, is the tax-deferred annuity, which compounds the amounts you invest, tax-free, until you begin making monthly withdrawals. The tax-deferred *fixed* annuity compounds your savings at a fixed percentage rate, which is guaranteed for a year or more. The tax-deferred *variable* annuity invests your savings in your choice of mutual funds. Annuities are sometimes favored by older individuals because, like life insurance contracts, they bypass probate and the proceeds are immediately paid to the beneficiary named in the policy.

How is the monthly amount determined? The amount you will receive each month is determined by the following factors: your age when you begin monthly withdrawals (a process that goes by the technical name of annuitization), the withdrawal option you select, and the amount of money invested.

How does age affect the monthly amount? When you purchase life insurance, the insurance company bases the annual premium you pay on the number of years you're expected to live—the younger you are, the less of a risk you are, and the lower the premiums. Annuities are the reverse of life insurance—the younger you are, the longer you're likely to live, and the more payments you're likely to receive. Consequently, assuming the same investment, your monthly payments will be higher if you begin to annuitize at age 75 than they would be if you began at age 70.

What are your withdrawal options and how do they affect the monthly amount? Just as age affects the monthly payment, so does your choice of withdrawal options. Your monthly payment is decreased if your annuity covers both you and your spouse and/or if you desire a guaranteed number of payments (period certain) rather than a lifetime annuity in which payments terminate at death. Your options are the following:

Fixed period annuity—You receive monthly payments for a set number of years.

Fixed amount annuity—You receive a set monthly amount until your principal is exhausted.

Life annuity—You receive a monthly income that terminates at your death.

Joint life and last survivor annuity—You and your spouse receive a monthly income that terminates when the second spouse dies (monthly payments are lower than a life annuity because two lives are covered). If your company purchases the annuity, you must select this option unless your spouse provides written consent to another form of payment.

Life annuity with period certain—You receive a lifetime income that is guaranteed for a minimum number of years (usually ten or twenty). If you die before the guaranteed time period has elapsed, your beneficiary will continue to receive payments for the remaining number of years specified.

How are your payments taxed? It depends on how much of the principal amount consists of before-tax dollars. If, for example, you or your company purchases the annuity with the proceeds of a pension plan to which you did not contribute, all of the payments you receive will be taxable. If you contributed after-tax dollars to your company pension or purchased the annuity with after-tax dollars, part of each payment will be taxable and part will be tax-free. Your benefits counselor, insurance agent, or accountant can provide you with tax information.

The decision as to which, if any, annuity is right for you, is governed by many factors. Use the following "Dos" as a guide.

• DO find out what expenses are involved in purchasing an annuity. Most annuities are no-load policies, meaning that all of your investment goes to work for you. Some policies, however, charge a sales load of 5% or more. Are there any annual costs or fees? Some annuities (particularly variable policies) impose annual management and mortality (to guarantee return of your principal investment at death) fees that will reduce your annual return by at least 1.5%. If you change your mind about annuitizing and decide to withdraw your money in a lump sum, what penalties will be charged? Some policies will allow you to withdraw 6% to 10% of your principal each year at no cost but will deduct a declining charge (6% the first year, 5% the second, etc.) for withdrawals in excess of that amount.

• DO find out what rate your money will earn. If you're considering purchasing a deferred annuity and plan to withdraw your funds or annuitize at a future date, ask the agent what rate of interest your money will earn and for how long. If interest rates rise in the future, will your earnings keep pace (if rates rise, say, 2% in the next year or two, how much increase in yield can you expect)? If the rate on your policy is lowered, can you cash it in without penalty? What minimum rate is guaranteed? Get this information in writing.

• DO find out how safe your money will be. If you're buying a lifetime income, you want the company to be around for the rest of your life. Deal only with companies that are licensed to sell policies in New York (their requirements are among the most stringent) and that show you literature rating them as A or A+ by A. M. Best Co., an independent company that rates insurers.

• DO compare at least four companies before you invest. You'll be surprised at the difference in monthly payments, given the same amount and choice of withdrawal options. While the annual return on your investment may be two or three percentage points higher than from other guaranteed investments, remember that, once you annuitize, you never get your principal back. If you purchase a deferred annuity and plan to annuitize in several years, the amount of monthly payment will be determined at the time you annuitize. Should you become dissatisfied with the annuity you select, you can then withdraw the proceeds (you'll be subject to a 5% IRS penalty if you're under 59½ and have held the contract for less than ten years) or transfer your proceeds to another company's annuity, without tax consequence, if it pays a higher return. Most insurance companies do, however, charge a declining percentage of the proceeds for withdrawal during the first six to ten years. Once you begin annuitizing, your income will not change. To compare rates, consult the *Retirement Income Guide*, published twice a year by A. M. Best Company (Ambest Road, Oldwick, NJ 08858) and available at most libraries.

• DO compare withdrawal options before you make your choice. You'll come out ahead with an annuity if you and/or your spouse outlive the insurance company's actuarial life expectancies. For example, the life annuity option under which monthly payments terminate at your death may pay as much as 33% more each month than the joint-and-survivor option that pays the same monthly benefit for the lives of you and your spouse. If you're in good health and have a family history of longevity, it may be better for you to choose the life annuity and invest part of the difference so that the surviving spouse will have a nest egg when it's needed.

• DO compare the annuity with other investment choices. A 1982 study by National Education Association, based on policies that guaranteed an 11.5% return, indicated that over twelve years, the real yield (after expenses) was 8% for the best performer and only 0.5% for the worst. Many mutual funds allow automatic monthly withdrawals of the amount you desire. If the value of the fund rises, you can increase your withdrawal amount from time to time and still have more than your original investment. Because your income from an annuity is fixed, it won't keep pace with inflation as other investments are likely to do, and the money will eventually be gone. Unlike a bond, which returns your principal at maturity, an annuity runs out when you do. Be sure that the annual income you receive is at least 2% higher than you'd receive on a long-term bond investment, to compensate you for giving up your principal.

• DO purchase a fixed, rather than a variable, annuity. If you're buying a deferred annuity and plan to begin annuitizing at a later date, a fixed annuity guarantees a certain rate of return. The return on variable annuities, on the other hand, varies with investment results, so you're never certain of what rate you'll earn or what your account will be worth when it's time to withdraw (most insurers charge a mortality fee to guarantee you won't lose the money you invested if the value declines). The costs and risks involved are not worth the potential for a slightly greater yield.

Where Is Your Money?

Create and maintain an inventory of bank, savings, and securities accounts. One easy-to-follow format is offered here:

SAVINGS AND INVESTMENT ACCOUNT INVENTORY

Name of Institution	Address	Telephone
Account Holder(s)	Account Number	Type of Account
Contact Person	Hours	Remarks

Name of Institution	Address	Telephone
Account Holder(s)	Account Number	Type of Account
Contact Person	Hours	Remarks

Name of Institution	Address	Telephone
Account Holder(s)	Account Number	Type of Account
Contact Person	Hours	Remarks

Name of Institution	Address	Telephone
Account Holder(s)	Account Number	Type of Account
Contact Person	Hours	Remarks

**Worksheet 19:
What Is Your Personal
Situation?**

What percentage of your capital should be allocated to each vehicle? That depends upon the savings and investment profile that reflects your unique personal and financial situation. Circle the choice in each category below that best describes you. If most of your choices fall to the left of center, your investment portfolio can include up to 50% of income-producing equities, such as dividend-paying common or preferred stocks. If most of your choices fall to the right of center, you should stick with savings vehicles, notes, mortgages, and bonds.

WORKSHEET 19

Your Savings and Investment Profile

Safe	Safer	Safest
50% Loaned	75% Loaned	100% Loaned
50% Owned	25% Owned	

Income

More than $50,000	$25,000 to $50,000	Less than $25,000

Number of Family Members

One	Two	More than two

Age

50–65	66–75	76+

Level of Income Required for Living Expenses

Saving more than 5% of income	Saving 0–5% of income	Spending capital

Health

Good to excellent	Fair to good	Poor to fair

Attitude Toward Risk

Comfortable with risk	Able to tolerate some risk	Dislike risk

YOUR PROFILE   _____% LOANED   _____% OWNED

**Worksheet 20:
Where Should You Invest?**

Using your profile, you can determine how and where to invest by completing Worksheet 20. In Column 1 enter the current values of your savings and investments. Enter the total amounts of loaned and owned vehicles on Lines 1 and 2 and the total value of your savings and investments on Line 3. Then determine each investment's percentage of the total by dividing each entry in Column 1 by the value on Line 3 (use your calculator's memory function) and enter these figures in Column 2. Don't feel the need to make any changes if your percentages reveal a safer portfolio than your profile indicates. You can't be too safe. On the other hand, if the proportions indicate too much risk— such as 50% loaned and owned when you should have 100% loaned, consider shifting some of your riskier assets to safer vehicles. In the future, before you make an investment decision, run it through this worksheet to make certain that its effect on your profile will fit your needs.

WORKSHEET 20

Your Savings and Investment Portfolio

	(C1) Amount	(C2) % of L3
Savings Vehicles and Loaned Investments		
Savings vehicles (Bank and savings accounts, money market funds, etc.)	_____	_____
Short-term loaned investments (mature in one to three years)	_____	_____
Intermediate-term loaned investments (mature in three to ten years)	_____	_____
Long-term loaned investments (mature in more than ten years)	_____	_____
(L1) Total Savings and Loaned Investments	_____	_____
Owned Investments		
Dividend-paying stocks	_____	_____
Real estate equity (excluding residence) (real property, REITs)	_____	_____
Gold (gold-mining stocks, coins, bullion)	_____	_____
Other (business interests, antiques, etc.)	_____	_____
(L2) Total Owned Investments	_____	_____
(L3) Total Savings and Investments **(L1 + L2)**	_____	__100%__

Sample: Cyril Balsam

After completing worksheet 19, Cyril Balsam, an 81-year-old widower with an annual income of $10,000, remarked, "Even at this stage of the game, I'd like to have some fun with my money, but I don't want to take any unnecessary chances."

SAMPLE WORKSHEET 19:

Cyril Balsam's Savings and Investment Profile

Safe	Safer	Safest
50% Loaned	75% Loaned	100% Loaned
50% Owned	25% Owned	
Income		
More than $50,000	$25,000 to $50,000	(Less than $25,000)
Number of Family Members		
(One)	Two	More than two
Age		
50–65	66–75	(76+)
Level of Income Required for Living Expenses		
Saving more than 5% of income	Saving 0–5% of income	(Spending capital)
Health		
Good to excellent	Fair to good	(Poor to fair)
Attitude Toward Risk		
Comfortable with risk	(Able to tolerate some risk)	Dislike risk

YOUR PROFILE   _90_ % LOANED   _10_ % OWNED

Cyril considers his health to be poor because he suffers from arthritis and gout, and his need for spendable capital as well as his age put him in the "safest" category. After consulting the information on how to create a diversified portfolio with less than $10,000 (see pages 143–45) Cyril decided to invest $5,000 (about 8% of his savings capital) in a dividend-paying stock mutual fund. "I've always wanted to play the market," Cyril joked. "If I don't do it now, I may never get the chance!" He also shifted some of his savings to higher-yielding two-year certificates of deposit that will pay him more monthly income without exposing him to additional risk.

SAMPLE WORKSHEET 20:

Cyril Balsam's Savings and Investment Portfolio

	(C1) Amount	(C2) % of L3
Savings Vehicles and Loaned Investments		
Savings vehicles (Bank and savings accounts, money market funds, etc.)	40,000	67%
Short-term loaned investments (mature in one to three years)	15,000	25%
Intermediate-term loaned investments (mature in three to ten years)		
Long-term loaned investments (mature in more than ten years)		
(L1) Total Savings and Loaned Investments	55,000	92%
Owned Investments		
Dividend-paying stocks	5,000	8%
Real estate equity (excluding residence) (real property, REITs)		
Gold (gold-mining stocks, coins, bullion)		
Other (business interests, antiques, etc.)		
(L2) Total Owned Investments	5,000	8%
(L3) Total Savings and Investments (L1 + L2)	60,000	100%

Planning Your Estate

OBJECTIVE: To preserve your assets and protect your loved ones. How do you want your assets to be distributed? Do you want to make special bequests to charitable institutions or valued friends? What should be done if you become unable to manage your affairs? How can you avoid federal estate taxes?

WHAT YOU WILL NEED

    Copies of wills and trusts

As you approach the end of your journey in this world, the ones you care for may still have some distance to travel. The effective planning of your estate can preserve its value, ensure that your assets are distributed according to your wishes, and prevent family discord. Many people postpone estate planning because they equate it with the unpleasant thought of death. But estate planning really has to do with keeping alive the pleasure that can be derived from the money you've saved and the possessions you've enjoyed acquiring. If you're one of those who doesn't care what happens to your assets after you're gone, you should know that by choosing not to have an estate plan you are making a less desirable choice. Your assets *must* be disposed of in some way. If you don't have a will or other estate plan, your assets will be subject to the will (the laws) of your home state. Generally, state laws mandate distribution of your assets to your closest relatives, whoever they may be. If you want to donate some of your assets to your church or favorite charity or to a special or needy friend, make these arrangements now, and enjoy the peace of mind and assurance that your money will be utilized in the best possible way.

An attorney who specializes in estate planning can help you determine the best ways to hold title to your assets and arrange for estate transfer. It will save you money in legal fees if you understand the choices you have—and their consequences—before you schedule an appointment. Your meeting with an attorney should focus on two major concerns: how you should hold title to your assets, and what your estate planning concerns are. The series of questions listed here should help you prepare for your meeting.

How Should You Hold Title to Your Assets?

The way you hold title to your assets can speed up the distribution of your estate, eliminate the necessity of court proceedings (called probate), and reduce estate taxes—but it can also result in your assets falling into the wrong hands. The following questions will point out the benefits and pitfalls of various forms of ownership.

1.   Holding title to assets in your own name simply means that you are the sole owner and the disposition of those assets at death is determined by the instructions in your will or by the laws of "intestacy" in your state if you do not have a will. All assets that are held in your name alone will be included in your probate estate.

Which assets should you hold in your own name? _____

_____

_____

2.   Certain types of assets, such as banking, checking, and savings accounts and certificates of deposit, that are held in joint tenancy with right of survivorship are owned by two individuals (in this case, a husband and wife), and either owner can make decisions as to management and sale of the assets. Many couples choose to set up bank and savings accounts in this way. When one owner dies, the assets automatically become the sole property of the survivor. This can be an ideal arrangement between spouses when both are healthy and Medicaid eligibility is not a lurking issue and when the total estate is valued at less than $600,000. If the estate is worth more, it can create an unnecessary tax liability.

Which assets should you hold in joint tenancy with right of survivorship (JTWROS) with your spouse? _____

_____

_____

3.   Putting title to your assets in joint tenancy with a friend or relative (other than your spouse) can have far-reaching implications. First, putting assets into joint tenancy with anyone other than your spouse can create a liability for federal gift tax (if the value of the estate exceeds $600,000) because you are actually making a gift of half the value of the assets (there is no gift tax liability for gifts between spouses). Second, your co-tenant may be able to control or sell the joint asset against your wishes, subject to the liens of creditors. Third, if your co-tenant predeceases you, you may have to pay state inheritance taxes to get back the asset. Finally, you may be inadvertently creating an unequal division of your estate. Even if your will instructs otherwise, assets held in joint tenancy become the sole property of the joint tenant when you die. Speak with an attorney before you put anyone else's name on your property.

Which assets should you hold in joint tenancy with right of survivorship (JTWROS) with anyone other than your spouse? _____

_____

_____

_____

4.   Stocks, bonds, and real property registered in joint tenancy can be sold or transferred only if both tenants sign. If the other owner will not consent to sale or is unable to consent because of illness or incapacity (and you do not have a valid power of attorney), you may not be able to sell, even though the assets were yours originally. There are relatively simple legal proceedings to free a home for sale by the healthy spouse, but for other assets, these warnings apply.

Which assets should not be held in joint tenancy? _____

_____

_____

_____

5.   A durable power of attorney does not involve transfer of ownership of your assets, but it does empower someone else to take charge of your assets only if you become incompetent or unable to manage them yourself. If you have no spouse, rather than putting a child's name on your bank or brokerage accounts, thus transferring part ownership, your purpose may be better accomplished by granting one of your children or a trusted friend a power of attorney. That person then may withdraw funds, if needed. At death, the remaining assets in the accounts will be distributed according to the instructions in your will.

Which assets should be covered by a durable power of attorney?

_____

_____

_____

6. Bank and savings accounts and Series EE U.S. Savings Bonds can be registered: "Your Name as trustee for Child's Name." This is not a real trust in which you, the trustee, are legally responsible for managing the assets of your child. Nor is this like a joint tenancy in which you've made a gift and given up control of the account. The words "as trustee for" really mean "payable at death to." Accounts registered in this manner can be an effective way to transfer assets to children if the estate value is less than $600,000. If you wish to divide your estate equally between, say, three children, you can maintain three separate accounts of equal value, each in trust for one child. You maintain ownership and control of the accounts as long as you're alive. This is not, however, a good way to hold accounts with your spouse, if you want him or her to have access to the funds. A joint tenant account should be used for this purpose.

Which assets should be held "in trust for" someone else? _____

_____

_____

_____

7. During life, assets held as joint tenants in common are treated much the same as those held in JTWROS. When one owner dies, however, the property does not automatically become the sole property of the surviving owner(s). The deceased's share is disposed of according to his or her will instructions. Tenancy in common ownership is best suited to property that you own with someone who is not related—a business associate or friend, for example. The ownership interests do not have to be equal or limited to two people. There may be several co-tenants with various percentages of ownership. This form of ownership is not generally suited to property held by husband and wife if the couple's estate is worth less than $600,000 and each spouse desires that the assets become the property of the survivor.

Which assets should be held as tenants in common? _____

_____

_____

_____

8. If you live in Arizona, California, Idaho, Louisiana, New Mexico, Nevada, Texas, or Washiangton, assets held as community property are treated the same as property held as tenants in common (see #6, above). On the death of either spouse, half of community property goes to the surviving spouse, and disposition of the other half is determined by the deceased's will instructions. In addition, any property acquired during the marriage (other than an inheritance) that is registered in the name of one spouse will be treated as owned half by the husband and half by the wife. If you want these assets to go to your spouse automatically (and your estate is worth less than $600,000), it's best to own them as joint tenants with right of survivorship.

Which assets should be held as community property? _____

_____

_____

_____

9. For many people, the word "trust" conjures up visions of a Scrooge-like banker who reluctantly doles out money, a penny at a time. This is not the case. A trust is simply an arrangement under which one person controls property for the benefit of another, and it has many uses and benefits. An inter vivos (living) trust can be used to avoid the expenses and delays of legal probate proceedings so that your property passes, without delay, to your beneficiaries. If your estate is worth more than $600,000, the correct use of a testamentary trust (established by will at death) can save thousands of dollars in federal estate taxes. If your estate is relatively small (less than $100,000), and you want it all to go to your spouse when you die, ownership as joint tenants with right of survivorship will accomplish your purpose. If you're concerned, however, that your spouse or other beneficiaries may not be capable of managing the assets prudently, or that your spouse will remarry and your children might wind up with nothing, consider a trust arrangement.

Which assets should be held in a trust? _____

_____

_____

_____

What Are Your Estate-Planning Concerns?

1. Your spouse or other close family member or friend is the most likely candidate to serve as executor of your estate. The executor's responsibilities include taking inventory of your assets, arranging for property appraisals, engaging an attorney, paying funeral bills and other final expenses, and managing the estate assets until they're distributed. If you don't want to place this responsibility on a family member or feel that the family member might need expert assistance, you can appoint a bank trust department as executor or co-executor.

Who will you name as executor of your estate? _____

_____

_____

2. Who do you want to receive your assets? Your spouse? Your children or grandchildren? Other relatives or friends? Someone to whom you owe a debt of gratitude? Do you want to leave anything to your church, alma mater, hospital, or favorite charity or another needy institution? You must provide for these specific bequests in order to be certain that they'll be carried out.

Who will be the beneficiaries of your estate? _____

_____

_____

_____

_____

3. If the value of your estate exceeds $600,000 and you have no spouse, the amount of your estate in excess of $600,000 will be subject to federal estate tax, starting at a rate of 37%. You can reduce the tax by making annual gifts of up to $10,000 in cash or property to as many people as you wish. For example, if you have four children, you can give each of them $10,000, reducing your estate by $40,000 each year. If you have a spouse, you can give each child double the amount as a joint gift, without tax consequence. If you own property that's likely to increase in value, making a gift of it removes the future appreciation from your estate.

Do you want to give away part of your estate now to reduce future taxes? _____

4. Do you have handicapped or disabled relatives who need your financial support? Do you want to provide a college fund for a grandchild? If one of your children is financially secure and another can't make ends meet, how can you make an equitable distribution? Many family disputes arise out of children's feelings that their parents made an unfair distribution of their assets. To avoid future conflict, it may be wise to discuss your estate plan with your children so that they understand the reasons behind your decisions.

How will your assets be divided among your beneficiaries? _____

_____

_____

5. If you want to disinherit a child (or grandchild, if the parents are deceased), excluding the child from your will won't prevent him or her from getting your assets. Depending on which state's law applies to your estate, you must specifically disinherit the child in your will. Otherwise, your child can claim the same percentage of your assets that he or she would be entitled to under state law if you died without a will. It is more difficult, however, to exclude your spouse. Depending upon the state in which you live, your spouse can lay claim to one-third to one-half of your estate, even if you specifically exclude him or her. However, your spouse can sometimes waive this right before you die (this is often done as part of a prenuptial agreement), or you can minimize the chances that the court will automatically protect your spouse. Consult an attorney.

Do you want to exclude one or more of your children or your spouse from your will? _____

_____

_____

6. Do you have specific items of personal property, such as heirlooms or antiques, that you want to go to someone special? Be sure to include a complete description of the item in your will.

Which items do you want to bequeath and to whom? _____

_____

_____

_____

7. You have the power to bring sight to the sightless and life to those whose heart, kidneys, or other vital organs can no longer sustain them. Corneal and organ transplants must be performed quickly when the time comes, so be certain that your loved ones know of your desire to help others, so that they can grant consent upon your demise. Obtain an eye and organ bequest form from your local Lion's Club and carry it in your wallet.

Do you want to make a gift of life or sight to someone? _____

8. While many physicians are sensitive to the whole patient's needs, some view it as their responsibility to sustain life even if the patient is hopelessly ill and faces unrelievable suffering. You can sign a "living will," sometimes called a "health care declaration," to confirm in writing for your doctors that you do not want medical treatment continued when you have no prospect of recovery. Many states have enacted legislation specifically authorizing such declarations. However, you should be wary of signing any preprinted form/document without consulting someone expert in the field, for you may be signing away important rights. In the view of many experts in this field, it would be better to sign a durable power of attorney designating an individual to make medical decisions on your behalf and the scope of authority they should have.

Do you want life-support treatment discontinued if there is no hope for recovery? _____

9. Prepaid funerals are a growing trend. They allow you to comparison shop and choose precisely the types of services you desire. They also free your loved ones of having to make decisions under the stress of bereavement. By knowing in advance how much it will cost, you can also make certain that funds are available when needed and avoid additional expense. If you're reluctant to plan in advance because you may change your mind later, find out if the plan is revocable or if prepayment is required. Many states require funeral homes to refund 100% of the money contributed for a prepaid plan, no questions asked, if you want to make other arrangements.

Do you want to make funeral arrangements in advance? _____

10. The average price of an adult's funeral today is $2,656, not including the plot or gravestone. A cremation, on the other hand, can cost less than a hundred dollars. The Neptune Society, a national organization with many local affiliates, performs low-cost cremations and can arrange to have the ashes scattered at sea. Consider which is best for you and your close ones, both emotionally and financially. Another alternative is donating your body to a medical school or hospital for research. You may be instrumental in helping to find a cure for a dread disease.

Do you want your body cremated or donated to medical research?

_____

_____

In the Event of an Emergency

Have you set up a plan of action to be carried out in the event of illness or accident? What if you were suddenly unable to manage your affairs or make decisions—who would step in and assume responsibility? Use the letter of instructions that follows to identify the person(s) whom you want to take charge of your affairs and provide instructions as to how you want those affairs handled. Keep a copy of this letter with your personal effects, make sure you inform a household member or trusted person of its whereabouts, and give copies to those who will be responsible for implementing your requests.

Your Letter of Instructions

Who will be responsible for carrying out these instructions?

Name _____

Address _____

Telephone _____ Day _____ Evening

If that person is unable to fulfill this responsibility, who is your second choice?

Name _____

Address _____

Telephone _____ Day _____ Evening

Does anyone hold a power of attorney that allows them to make decisions on your behalf? _____ If so,

who? _____

Address and telephone number, if not listed above: _____

_____

Hospital preference _____

Physician (name, address, phone) _____

_____

Location of health insurance policies _____

Location of life insurance policies _____

Insurance agent (name and phone) _____

_____

Medicare card location & number _____

Attorney (name, address, phone) _____

_____

Other persons to be notified (name, address, phone)

_____

_____

_____

In what order should financial resources be withdrawn (bank, savings, money market, and
securities accounts—institution, account number, location of checkbook or statements)?   Order

_____   ____

_____   ____

_____   ____

Other resources

_____   ____

_____   ____

_____   ____

What other information should be known or instructions carried out (e.g., care of pets, location and
combinations or keys to safes or safety deposit boxes, hidden assets)?

_____

_____

_____

Location of Living Will

_____

Disposition of eyes and organs

_____

BURIAL INSTRUCTIONS

Funeral home

_____

Name   Address   Phone

Location of burial plot _____

Final disposition instructions _____

DISPOSITION OF PERSONAL PROPERTY

Description of Item	Location	Disposition

Remarks

_____

_____

_____

_____

Your Financial Plan

OBJECTIVE: To put it all together and stay on course. Should you need help with your financial planning, who can you turn to for advice and assistance? How can you make certain that your plan will adjust to your changing circumstances?

WHAT YOU WILL NEED
 Completed worksheets

Now that you've completed all the steps necessary to ensure a safe journey, you'll want to make it easy to stay on the right track. By completing the worksheets in this book, you've created your own personal financial planning workbook. Consider copying your worksheets and inserting them in a three-ring binder so that you can easily refer to them in the future, making changes or updating your financial plan as your needs and goals change. If you have an annual income of $25,000 or more, an investable net worth in excess of $50,000, or desire professional assistance with your financial planning, you should consider engaging the services of a financial planner before implementing the decisions that you've made through completing the worksheets.

Selecting a Financial Planner

A financial planner is an individual who can help you evaluate your present financial condition, identify tax reduction strategies, select an investment portfolio, and plan your estate transfer. In short, the function of the financial planner is to assist you in completing the steps outlined in this workbook and advise you as to the best course of action for your personal situation. Because financial planning is a relatively

173

new field, many of those who call themselves financial planners may not be qualified to help you. Planners are listed in the telephone directory under "Financial Planners," but the best way to choose one is by personal recommendation. Ask your accountant, attorney, and bank officer for names of individuals they've worked with. If you have any friends or relatives who have engaged the services of a planner, get their feedback, too. You should also write or call the International Association for Financial Planning (IAFP) at 5775 Peachtree-Dunwoody Road, Suite 120-C, Atlanta, GA 30342 (404-252-9600), and the Institute for Certified Financial Planners (ICFP) at 10065 E. Harvard Avenue, Suite 320, Denver, CO 80231-5942 (303-751-7600). These two professional organizations can provide you with the names of qualified planners in your area.

Don't put your trust in a planner who promises to make you rich or solve your money problems with some unique investment or strategy. Like healers who promote miracle cures, planners who tout financial panaceas must be avoided. No one can predict future investment performance or tax law changes, and many people have lost fortunes looking for that pot of gold.

Financial planners who provide investment advice are required to register as Investment Advisers with the Securities and Exchange Commission. A planner who calls himself or herself a Registered Investment Adviser has completed the application forms and paid a fee. No test of competency or demonstration of proficiency is needed. If you've engaged a financial planner who you believe has misrepresented either the services or the investment he or she offers, contact the Office of Consumer Affairs, Securities and Exchange Commission, 450 Fifth Street NW, Washington, DC 20549, (202-272-7440). They will ensure that you get assistance in a convenient location.

Questions to Ask a Financial Planner

Now that you've completed your financial plan, you'll want to be certain that it continues to work for you. Before you engage the services of a planner, interview at least three or four. If you're not satisfied with their responses to the questions below, interview others.

1. What is your background and experience? _____

_____

_____

The planner should have a college degree and experience in one or more of the financial fields: accounting, economics, business administration, finance, investments, insurance, and law. Generally, the planner's strength will lie in his or her area of education and training. A planner who's a CPA, for example, can be expected to be well versed in income and estate taxes, while a stockbroker planner should know more about investments.

2. Do you consult with other professionals? _____

_____

Some planning firms employ individuals with different backgrounds to provide the necessary expertise. If the firm has a CPA, accountant, insurance specialist, investment adviser, and estate planning attorney on its full-time staff, you're likely to get a better plan than you would from an individual who does all the work alone. If the planner works alone, ask if he or she calls on specialists in other fields for assistance.

3. What degrees or designations do you hold? _____

_____

There are no laws or regulations to prevent any person from opening an office and calling himself or herself a financial planner. While a degree doesn't ensure competence, it at least indicates the person's willingness to achieve a level of professionalism. In addition to an undergraduate degree, many planners have completed the accredited financial planning curriculum offered by the College of Financial Planning (graduates earn the Certified Financial Planner or CFP designation) or the American College (which grants the Chartered Financial Consultant designation, or ChFC).

4. Can you provide references? _____

_____

Ask for the names of at least three individuals who would be willing to attest to the planner's competence. Request the name of at least one client whose situation is similar to yours.

5. Can I examine a sample plan? _____

_____

Find out if you can have a copy of a plan for an older client or one whose situation is similar to yours. Is it easy to understand? Do the recommendations make sense? Does it seem to be in tune with that person's specific needs and goals? Many plans are computerized printouts and projections that rehash the same recommendations for everyone, with only minor variations. Be sure you'll get a plan that's uniquely yours.

6. Whom will I be working with? _____

Some planners employ assistants who gather your personal data and research information. Find out whom you'll be working with, right from the start.

7. What steps are involved in the financial planning process? _____

_____

_____

Usually, at least two meetings are scheduled—one introductory interview and a second data-gathering session. The planner may also need to contact your attorney and accountant for additional information. You should be presented with a completed plan within four to six weeks after the planner has compiled all the necessary data, and it should be reviewed once a year or when there are any changes in your financial situation.

8. What sources do you use for investment and insurance recommendations? _____

_____

_____

Does the planner do the research or rely on an independent research company or investment and insurance publications? Ask to see some of the planner's advisory materials to determine that they are both objective and adequately researched. Planners who are employed by brokerage or insurance firms may sell only their company's products, which may not be the best for you.

9. How will the plan recommendations be implemented? _____

_____

_____

Will the planner institute the steps that are needed to put your plan into action? Will he or she purchase investments and insurance for you, complete your tax return, draw up a will or trust? If not, does the planner provide specific recommendations and directions so that you can implement the recommendations yourself?

10. How much will it cost? _____

Fee-only planners charge an hourly fee, which usually ranges from $50 to $200. The planner should be able to give you an estimate of how long it will take and how much it will cost. Generally, a customized plan costs from $750 to $2,000 or more for a wealthy individual. Commission planners charge no fees but earn sales commissions on the products—insurance, annuities, mutual funds, limited partnerships—they recommend to implement the plan. Most planners who are employed by brokerage firms work on a commission basis. Fee-plus-commission planners charge a combination of fee and commission. Which is best? While the fee-only planner's services may appear more costly, such planners are likely to recommend products that have no built-in sales charges, so you may come out ahead because of the commission savings. The fee-only planner may also be more objective, because his or her income doesn't depend upon selling you something. The services of the commission planner, on the other hand, cost nothing and may be just as good as those of the fee planner. How a planner is compensated is not as important a consideration as his or her knowledge, integrity, and concern for your best interests. Like other successful business and professional people, good planners want satisfied clients.

Maintaining Your Financial Planning Schedule

Worksheet	Recommended Review or Update	Most Recent Update
1—Your Starting Point	Annually	_____
2—Is Your Money Working As Hard As It Should?	Annually	_____
3—How Did You Get Here?	Four times a year	_____
4—Your Monthly Income	Monthly	_____
5—Your Monthly Expenses	Monthly	_____
6—Are You Staying on Course?	Monthly	_____
7—How Much Will Your Money Grow?	Semiannually	_____
8—How Much Can You Afford to Spend Each Month?	Semiannually	_____
9—Can You Put Your Home Equity to Work?	When you plan a housing change	_____
10—Should You Own or Rent Your Home?	When you plan a housing change	_____
11—Compare Before You Buy	Annually	_____
12—Evaluate Your Home Insurance Protection	Semiannually	_____
13—Evaluate Your Automobile Insurance Protection	Semiannually	_____
14—Your Household and Personal Inventory	Monthly	_____
15—What Are Your Projected Tax Liability and Tax Rate?	Each October (year-end planning)	_____
16—Do You Qualify for the Credit for the Elderly or Disabled?	Each October (year-end planning)	_____
17—Select the Best Savings Vehicles	Semiannually	_____
18—Select the Best Investments	Semiannually	_____
19—Your Savings and Investment Profile	Semiannually	_____
20—Your Savings and Investment Portfolio	Semiannually	_____
Your Letter of Instructions	Annually	_____

Now that you've completed this guidebook, take some time to relax and review the plan you've created. Enjoy contemplating the fruitful years that lie ahead, knowing that you're as prepared as you can be for any financial obstacle. You've put the wheels in motion for a secure financial journey, as long as you live.

Investment Digest

Certificates of Deposit (CDs)

Time deposits issued by banks and savings and loans. CDs range in maturity from two weeks to ten years, depending on the sponsoring institution. Interest may be paid monthly, quarterly, semiannually, or at maturity. A penalty is charged for withdrawal prior to maturity.

Where to buy: Banks, savings and loans, some brokerage firms.
Price stability: The price remains stable.
Taxability: Interest is fully taxable.
Minimum purchase: $100.
Transaction costs: None.

Common Stock

A security that represents equity ownership in a company. Each common stockholder is entitled to vote on company policy, share in the company's profits (via receipt of dividends), and participate in the increase or decrease of the company's value (rise or fall in the stock price). The largest companies trade on the New York Stock Exchange and prices are listed in the financial section of your daily newspaper under the heading "New York Stock Exchange Stocks."

Where to buy: Brokerage firms and some banks.
Price stability: Prices can fluctuate widely due to changes in the economy and the fortunes of the company.
Taxability: Dividends and profits from appreciation are generally fully taxable.
Minimum purchase: One share; however the minimum transaction charge of $25 to $30 makes a one-share purchase unfeasible.

Transaction costs: Depending upon number of shares and dollar amount of purchase or sale, approximately 1% to 2% of investment. Discount brokerage firms, which provide no investment research or advice, charge about one-half the amount of full-service brokerage firms.

Corporate Bonds, Notes, and Debentures

IOUs issued by corporations. Bonds and notes are backed by collateral and differ only in length of maturity—notes usually mature in less than five years, bonds in five years or more. Debentures are backed by the faith and credit of the company and are usually issued by well-known, financially sound companies. As a bondholder, you are a creditor of the firm, a safer position than that of the stockholder. Prices of actively traded bonds of large companies are listed in the financial section of your daily newspaper under "New York Stock Exchange Bonds." Interest is paid semiannually.

Where to buy: Brokerage firms and some banks.

Price stability: Between issue and maturity date, bond prices will be affected by changes in current interest rates. If interest rates fall, the prices of outstanding bonds will rise to adjust to the new interest rate environment. If rates rise, the prices of outstanding bonds will fall.

Taxability: Interest is taxable. If the bond is sold for more than you paid, the profit is taxable.

Minimum purchase: One bond ($1,000).

Transaction costs: If the bond is purchased when it's issued, there are no transaction costs. The cost to buy and sell outstanding bonds is usually $10 per bond (1% of maturity value).

Government National Mortgage Association Certificates (GNMAs, Ginnie Maes)

U.S. government–backed pools of thirty-year fixed-rate mortgages, these are often referred to as Ginnie Maes. The yield is calculated on the basis of the mortgage rate and the length of time the mortgages are expected to be held, usually an average of twelve years. If interest rates fall, some or all of the mortgages are likely to be paid off earlier; if they rise, the mortgages will be held longer. Holders of GNMAs receive amortized monthly payments that are part interest and part return of principal. These are complex investments that are often advertised in a misleading way. Many GNMA ads are directed toward the senior citizen market and emphasize high yields and government guarantees. Ads that emphasize their government guarantee may not tell you the negatives: These are not actively traded securities (unless purchased within the framework of a mutual fund). If you need to sell early, you may not get a fair price. Like bonds, their values are affected by changing interest rates. If you buy a GNMA that's selling at a premium (meaning the price has risen since issue date because interest rates have dropped), it's likely that the underlying mortgages will be refinanced so that your investment will mature prematurely and you won't get all of your money back.

Where to buy: Brokerage firms and banks.

Price stability: Between issue and maturity date, prices will fluctuate with changing interest rates. As mortgages within the pool are paid down or refinanced, the price of the GNMA and its yield decline.

Taxability: Only the interest portion of the monthly payment you receive is taxable.

Minimum purchase: GNMA pools are priced at $25,000 but can be purchased in a unit trust or mutual fund for $1,000 or less.

Transaction costs: The cost is built in to the price of the pool so that the yield is based on your total investment. (See "Unit Trusts" and "Mutual Funds.")

Limited Partnerships

Investments in real estate, oil and gas properties, computers and aircraft, research and development of new products, and other ventures requiring a large amount of capital. The limited partnership form of ownership permits many individuals to pool their money for the purpose of investing in vehicles that are too costly and/or risky for one person alone. A general partner organizes the partnership and selects and manages the investments. The limited partners receive income, tax benefits (which were greatly curtailed under the Tax Reform Act of 1986), and potential profits when the partnership is liquidated. The word "limited" means that the investors' liability for losses incurred or legal actions arising from the partnership investments is limited to the amount of investment. You can lose all of the money you invest, but no more. When you buy a share of a partnership, you may be tying your money up for as long as thirty years. Moreover, the tax benefits that many partnerships emphasize can evaporate when tax laws change. And, if you need to sell early, you'll incur a substantial loss.

Where to buy: Financial planning and brokerage firms.

Price stability: There is no active market for resale of partnership units and no way you can ascertain a current value.

Taxability: Depending upon the investment within the partnership, there may be deductions for expenses and depreciation of property.

Minimum purchase: $5,000 per partnership interest.

Transaction costs: Commissions, acquisition, and management fees average 15% to 25% of the amount invested.

Municipal Bonds and Notes

IOUs issued by states and municipalities to finance public improvements. The interest they pay is not subject to federal income tax, but it's normally a lower rate than you'd receive on a taxable bond or note of the same maturity. Municipals are considered to be safer investments than corporate bonds, but there have been instances of default. You can also purchase insured municipal bonds. Their yield is ¼% to ½% lower than uninsured bonds, but they're worth the extra margin of safety. Because the municipal bond market is relatively inactive, you'll take a loss of 10% to 15% of your investment if you need to sell a bond prior to maturity.

Where to buy: Brokerage firms and some banks.

Price stability: The same as for corporate bonds and notes.

Taxability: Interest is exempt from federal income tax.

Minimum purchase: One bond ($1,000).

Transaction cost: $10 per bond (1% of par value).

Mutual Funds

Mutual funds are professionally managed portfolios of stocks, bonds, and/or money market vehicles. They offer investment diversification and ongoing management for an annual fee of ½% to 2%. Some investment companies sponsor several funds with various types of investments and objectives. These so-called fund families usually allow you to transfer your money from one fund to another at minimal or no cost. The most complete resource for mutual fund information is the *Weisenberger Investment Companies Service*, available at your public library. Several magazines, such as *Consumer Reports, Business Week, Changing Times, Forbes,* and *Money,* frequently run comparisons of mutual fund performance.

Where to buy: No-load mutual funds impose no sales charges and can be purchased directly from the investment company. Load funds impose sales charges of up to 9% of your invested capital and are generally purchased through intermediaries such as stockbrokers or financial planners.

Price stability: Depends upon the investments within the fund.

Taxability: Funds containing municipal bonds (tax-free bond funds) pay interest that's tax-exempt.

Minimum purchase: Usually $500 to $1,000 with subsequent additions of at least $1,000. A few funds have lower minimum purchase requirements.

Transaction costs: None for true no-load funds. For load funds, sales charges can run as high as 9% and may be deducted from either the purchase (front-end load) or sale (back-end load) price. Annual administration charges (called 12b-1 plans) may be as high as 1½%.

Preferred Stock

Corporate stock that pays a fixed dividend. The owner of a preferred issue may or may not have voting rights, depending upon the company. Many senior citizens invest in preferred stock because the dividend is higher and safer than that of the same company's common stock. However, the preferred stock's price and its dividend will not increase with the company's profits, while the common stock's price and dividend usually will, eventually outpacing the preferred. Preferred stock is also less actively traded than common stock, so you'll pay more when you buy and get less when you sell a preferred issue. Your stock may also be redeemed by the company if interest rates drop, so you'll have to reinvest your capital at lower rates and you may sustain a loss. Be certain to weigh the pros and cons carefully before you invest.

Where to buy: Brokerage firms and some banks.

Price stability: The same as for corporate bonds and notes.

Taxability: The dividend is taxable.

Minimum purchase: Same as common stock.

Transaction Costs: Same as common stock.

Series EE U.S. Savings Bonds

IOUs issued by the U.S. government to encourage saving. You can't withdraw the interest earned until the bond matures (or you cash it in), so that these are unsuitable investments for those needing current income. The interest is pegged to the rate paid on five-year U.S. Treasury notes, with a minimum guarantee of 6% (for bonds purchased since November 1, 1986) if the bond is held for five years or more. EEs mature when they double in value, a maximum of twelve years.

Where to buy: Savings institutions.

Price stability: There is no market for resale. If you cash in your bond before holding it five years, you'll receive less interest. If you cash it in after five years, you'll receive the interest earned to date.

Taxability: You may pay tax on the interest accrued each year or defer payment of taxes until the bond matures (or you cash it in).

Minimum purchase: $25

Transaction costs: None

Unit Trusts

Fixed portfolios of securities, usually corporate or municipal bonds or GNMAs. Like mutual funds, they provide diversification with a minimum investment ($1,000 per unit). Unlike mutual funds, they are not actively managed and the portfolio that is selected when the trust is created remains unchanged until the bonds and mortgages are redeemed or mature.

Where to buy: Brokerage firms and financial planners.

Price stability: Same as corporate bonds and notes.

Taxability: Interest paid by corporate or GNMA trusts is taxable; interest paid by municipal bond trusts is tax-exempt.

Minimum purchase: One unit ($1,000).

Transaction costs: Approximately 4% to 5% of investment ($40–$50 per unit).

There is no charge for sale and no management fees.

U.S. Treasury Securities

IOUs issued by the U.S. Treasury and backed by the full faith and credit of the U.S. government. Treasury bills mature in one year or less (issued in three-, six-, and twelve-month maturities); notes mature in one to ten years (issued in two-, three-, four-, five-, seven-, and ten-year maturities); and bonds mature in twenty and thirty years. Three- and six-month bills are auctioned weekly by the Federal Reserve.

Where to buy: Newly issued bills can be purchased during the auction directly from your Federal Reserve bank or the Bureau of the Public Debt, Department of the Treasury, 1435 G Street NW, Room 429, Washington, DC 20226. You can also buy them through your bank or brokerage firm.

Price stability: Same as corporate bonds and notes.

Taxability: Interest is federally taxable but nontaxable at state and local levels.

Minimum purchase: $10,000 for bills, $5,000 for two- or three-year notes, $1,000 for bonds and notes maturing in four years or more.

Transaction costs: None, if purchased through a Federal Reserve bank or the Bureau of Public Debt; $30 to $65 if purchased through a bank or brokerage firm.

Glossary of Financial Terms

accrued interest   See under **interest.**

all-risk   An insurance policy covering real or personal property against all losses except those specifically excluded. All-risk policies do *not* cover damage or loss caused by flood, earthquake, war, nuclear accidents, and normal wear and tear.

annual renewable term insurance   See under **insurance.**

annuity   A series of equal payments from a pool of money. The amount of the payment is often based upon the recipient's (annuitant's) life expectancy and terminates at death. The different types of annuities are:

    certain   An annuity that guarantees payment for a minimum time period, usually ten or twenty years.

    deferred   An insurance company contract that compounds earnings on a tax-deferred basis and does not begin making payments until a later date.

    fixed   A deferred annuity that compounds earnings at a fixed rate, usually pegged to a U.S. Treasury security interest rate.

    variable   A deferred annuity that's invested in one or more of your choice of mutual funds. Return depends upon performance of the fund(s).

appreciate   To grow or increase in value. Individuals buy stock and real estate investments with the hope that they will appreciate.

ask(ing) price   The price at which someone (a dealer) is willing to sell a security (the price the dealer is asking).

asset   What a company or individual owns. Property, investments, and savings are assets.

    cash equivalent   An asset that can be converted to cash without penalty or loss of principal. Bank and savings accounts and money market funds are cash equivalents.

current An asset that is cash or expected to be converted into cash within twelve months. Short-term certificates of deposit and U.S. Treasury bills are examples of current assets.

liquid An asset that can be converted to cash without penalty or loss of principal.

balance sheet An accounting statement that lists descriptions and values of an individual's or company's assets, liabilities, and net worth (assets minus liabilities). It's a snapshot of financial condition at a single point in time.

bear market A declining stock market.

beneficiary The person who is named to receive the proceeds of a life insurance policy, IRA account, certain other contracts, trust, or an estate.

bid price The price at which someone (a dealer) is willing to purchase a security such as a stock or bond.

big board A popular name for the New York Stock Exchange.

bond A debt security by which investors lend money to the issuer, who agrees to pay a stated rate of interest over a specific time period, at the end of which the original investment will be returned. For more comprehensive explanations than offered here see Appendix A.

convertible A bond that can be exchanged for a certain number of shares of common stock of the issuing corporation.

corporate A bond issued by a corporation to raise capital, usually for a term of from five to thirty years.

municipal A bond issued by a state or municipality to finance public improvements. The interest is usually not subject to federal income tax.

savings (Series EE U.S.) A bond issued by the U.S. government to encourage savings. Although the bond matures when the interest equals the amount of the original investment, it continues to earn interest until it is cashed in.

Treasury A bond issued by the U.S. Treasury to finance the public debt. It's backed by the full faith and credit of the U.S. government and its term is from five to thirty years.

zero coupon A bond issued at a large discount from the maturity (par) value ($1,000) by a corporation, municipality, or the U.S. government. Interest is accrued until the bond matures, when the interest plus original investment equals $1,000.

bond mutual fund See under **mutual fund.**

broker An agent who handles orders to buy and sell securities, commodities, real estate, or other property.

bull market An advancing stock market.

capital Cash in reserve, savings, and other property of value. A person who "spends capital" reduces his or her net worth.

capital gain (loss) Profit (loss) incurred from the sale of property or securities. If a piece of property is purchased for $1,000 and later sold for $1,500 ($500), the capital gain (loss) is $500.

cash equivalent See under **asset.**

cash surrender value The amount of money the owner of a life insurance policy would receive if he or she cashed in (surrendered) the policy. The amount received is reduced by any policy loans outstanding.

casualty insurance See **insurance, property and casualty.**

certified financial planner A financial planner who has successfully completed the educational testing and work experience requirements of the International Board of Standards and Practices of Certified Financial Planners (IBCFP) and has agreed to adhere to the IBCFP Code of Ethics.

chartered financial consultant A financial planner who has successfully completed the course of studies offered by the American College at Bryn Mawr, Pennsylvania.

co-insurance clause An insurance contract proviso that the insured be responsible for part of the loss. A homeowner's policy, for example, stipulates that if the home is insured for less than 80% of market value, the insured will bear the cost of part of the loss. Co-insurance clauses in major medical policies require the policyholder to pay up to 20% of expenses.

comfort zone The amount of risk one can take without feeling upset or uncomfortable. "Selling down to the sleeping point" means ridding yourself of investments that cause you to stay awake at night and worry.

comon stock See under **stock.**

compounding Interest earned on principal plus previously earned interest. Savings accounts and investments may compound daily, monthly, or annually.

consumer price index A statistical device that measures the increase in the cost of goods and services (cost of living); an inflation indicator.

convertible bond See under **bond.**

convertible term insurance See under **insurance.**

coordination of benefits A provision of group medical insurance policies which states that the policyholder can receive benefits only to the extent of medical expenses incurred and cannot profit by owning more than one policy.

corporate bond See under **bond.**

cost basis Generally, the original cost of an asset, but it may be adjusted for certain reasons. For assets that pass through an estate, the cost basis is the value on the date of death, not the original cost. If you buy a home for $50,000 and spend $10,000 to add a garage, the cost basis becomes $60,000. Only the costs of permanent improvements increase the cost basis. Costs for repairs or replacement do not.

current asset See under **asset.**

current liability See under **liability.**

decreasing term insurance See under **insurance.**

deduction An item that can be legally deducted from taxable income, estates, or gifts, thus reducing the amount of money that's subject to tax.

deferral Postponement of tax liability. Individual Retirement Accounts (IRAs) feature tax deferral because the income earned in the account isn't taxed until funds are withdrawn.

deferred annuity See under **annuity.**

depreciation Decline in value of an asset due to usage or the passage of time. Tax laws permit deductions for business equipment and investments, such as real estate, that are likely to depreciate.

discount 1. The sale of anything below its stated value. 2. The amount by which a bond sells below par value ($1,000).

discount rate See under **interest.**

dividend The payment designated by a company's board of directors to be distributed among the holders of outstanding shares of stock. On preferred stock, the amount of the dividend is fixed and doesn't change from year to year. On common stock, the dividend varies with the fortunes of the company and is usually increased if profits increase or omitted if business is poor.

dollar cost averaging A policy of investing the same amount of money at regular intervals. For example, an individual who buys $100 worth of stock every month will buy more shares when the price of the stock is low (assumed to be undervalued) and fewer shares when the stock's price is high (may be overpriced).

donee The person to whom a gift is made.

donor The person who makes a gift.

durable power of attorney See **power of attorney, durable.**

entitlement The benefits payable to a Social Security recipient starting with the year the participant elects to take these benefits.

equity Net worth; assets minus liabilities. The equity in a home is the current market value less the mortgage outstanding—the actual ownership value.

estate All assets owned by an individual at the time of death, including cash, personal effects, business interests, property, and investments.

estate planning The process of determining how one's estate will be dispersed. Estate planning can reduce taxes, avoid forced sale of assets at an importune time, minimize confusion and conflict, and ensure that loved ones are provided for.

executor The person(s) named by the one who writes a will to carry out the will instructions. May be a relative, friend, attorney, and/or financial institution.

fiduciary An executor, administrator, or trustee; one who has the responsibility of managing property for the benefit of others.

financial planner A person who designs and implements a financial plan. See also **certified financial planner; chartered financial consultant.**

financial planning The process of determining how one's money will be managed. Financial planning can reduce taxes and insurance costs, decrease spending, maximize investment return while minimizing risk, and ensure financial security.

fixed annuity See under **annuity.**

401(k) plan A tax-deferred savings plan available to employees of some corporations. You may contribute before-tax earnings through payroll deductions up to a maximum percentage set by the company, not to exceed $7,313 in 1988, adjusted for inflation thereafter. The company may match part or all of your contribution.

403(b) plan A tax-deferred savings plan available to employees of schools, colleges, hospitals, and other non-profit organizations. You may contribute up to 16⅔% of before-tax earnings (not to exceed $9,500 a year) through payroll deductions.

fully insured Regarding Social Security, a worker who has: (1) a minimum of six quarters' coverage with one quarter of coverage for each calendar year commencing one year after 1950 (or the quarter when the worker reaches age 21, if later) and ending one year before the worker dies, becomes disabled, or reaches age 62, whichever is the earliest or (2) at least thirty-seven quarters of coverage (in 1988).

gift tax A tax levied on the transfer of gift property. The tax is owed by the giver, or donor, not the recipient of the gift.

gift tax exclusion The right under the Internal Revenue Code to exclude from gift tax liability the first $10,000 given in a single year by one person to another. A husband and wife, for example, may give each of their four children $20,000 a year (a total of $80,000) without any gift tax liability. There is no tax on gifts between spouses.

growth mutual fund See under **mutual fund.**

income mutual fund See under **mutual fund.**

income statement A financial statement that summarizes income and expenses for a certain time period.

individual retirement account (IRA) A tax-deferred savings plan that may be established by any individual under age 70½ who has earned income (wages or salary). A person may contribute an amount equal to earnings, up to a maximum of $2,000 annually (plus $250 if a separate account is established for a spouse). Contributions are fully deductible from adjusted gross income (AGI) if (1) the contributor isn't covered by an employer's pension plan *or* (2) adjusted gross income (AGI) is less than $25,000 for a single person ($50,000 for a couple). If AGI is between $25,000 and $35,000 for a single person ($40,000 and $50,000 for a couple), the deduction is prorated. Deductible contributions aren't taxed until money is withdrawn, at age 59½ or later. Tax penalties are imposed for early withdrawal.

inflation An economic condition during which prices rise.

inflation guard endorsement A provision in a homeowner's policy that automatically increases the amount of coverage at regular intervals. It does not, however, guarantee that the property is completely protected, because inflation may rise more rapidly than the automatic increases.

insurance A method of eliminating or reducing the financial burden of serious events such as fire, accident, theft, illness, disability, and death.

    liability Insurance coverage that pays for losses incurred by others as a result of the actions or negligence of the insured. Umbrella liability is an excess liability policy that provides higher coverage ($1 million or more) than the other property and casualty policies owned.

    life A contract under which an insurance company agrees, in exchange for a specified amount (the premium), to pay a certain amount (the face value of the policy) to one or more persons (the beneficiaries of the policy) upon the death of the insured individual.

        annual renewable term (also known as ART, or term, insurance) A policy that's issued for the number of years stated in the contract, usually until age 65 or older, and is renewable annually at a predetermined premium (which increases each year as the insured becomes older and a greater risk), without a medical examination or evidence of insurability. It does not build cash value and can be cancelled at the option of the insured.

        convertible term Term life insurance that the insured can convert to whole life insurance without obtaining evidence of insurability.

        decreasing term A type of life insurance in which the benefit is reduced each month or year while the premium remains unchanged. Mortgage insurance, which covers a decreasing liability, is a decreasing term policy.

        single premium A type of whole life insurance that entails the payment of a single premium, usually a minimum of $5,000, and builds immediate cash value, which can be borrowed without tax consequence.

universal   A type of whole life insurance in which the cash value (savings account) portion of the policy builds at a rate tied to current market interest.

variable   A type of whole life insurance in which the cash value is invested in a mutual fund.

whole (also known as ordinary life, straight life, or cash value insurance)   A policy that combines term (pure) life insurance with an investment/savings account, so that the policy can be surrendered for cash or borrowed against.

property and casualty   Insurance coverage that provides for the repair or replacement of or compensation for property that has been lost, stolen, damaged, or destroyed.

interest   The payment that a borrower makes to a lender for the use of his or her money. Banks pay interest on bank accounts; companies pay interest on the bonds they issue.

accrued   Interest that has been earned but not received. If you sell a bond in between the semiannual interest payment dates, you will receive the interest you accrued up to the date of sale.

discount rate   The rate of interest the federal reserve bank charges its member banks to borrow money.

prime rate   The rate of interest banks charge their best customers to borrow money.

intestate   One who dies without leaving a valid will. The settlement of the estate is handled according to the laws of the deceased's state.

investment   An asset that may increase or decrease in value. Investments include stocks, bonds, real property, businesses, antiques, and collectibles.

investor   A person who purchases investments with the hope that they will produce a higher return than a savings account or other cash equivalent.

IRA   See **individual retirement account.**

joint tenants in common   Ownership of property by two or more people in such a manner that each person has an undivided interest that can be bequeathed at death.

joint tenants with right of survivorship   Ownership of property by two or more people in such a manner that when one owner dies, the remaining owner(s) gain(s) title to the property.

Keogh account   A tax-deferred savings plan available to self-employed persons and their employees under age 70½. Annual contributions to the plan are based on a percentage of earnings and are deductible from taxable income. Contributions and plan earnings are not taxed until money is withdrawn, at age 59½ or later. Tax penalties are imposed for early withdrawal.

leverage The use of borrowed funds to acquire an investment. Real estate investments are normally leveraged because the purchaser makes a down payment and finances the rest of the cost with a mortgage. Stocks acquired on margin (using fully-paid-for securities as collateral) are another form of leverage. Leverage entails risk because rising interest rates can increase the amount owed and the investment can decline in value.

liability What a company or individual owes; includes IOUs, debts, loans, mortgages, and other obligations.
> **current** a liability that comes due within the next twelve months.

liability insurance See under **insurance.**

life insurance See under **insurance.**

limited partner One who invests in a limited partnership and whose liability for losses incurred by the partnership is limited to the amount invested.

liquid asset See under **asset.**

load mutual fund See under **mutual fund.**

marital deduction The deduction allowed by the Internal Revenue Code from the deceased's gross estate for property that passes to the spouse. All property passing to a surviving spouse is excluded from estate tax liability.

marketability The ease with which an investment or asset can be bought or sold. Common stocks listed on the New York Stock Exchange are considered to be very marketable; real estate is considered to be poorly marketable.

market price The last reported price at which a stock or bond changed hands.

maturity The date on which a loan, bond, debenture, or certificate of deposit comes due and the principal is repaid.

money market account A savings account with a bank, credit union, or savings and loan that pays the money market rate of interest.

money market mutual fund See under **mutual fund.**

money market rate The rate of interest currently being paid on money market instruments (short-term U.S. government and bank securities, bank certificates of deposit, and commercial paper).

municipal bond See under **bond.**

mutual fund An investment company that invests shareholders' money in a diversified portfolio of securities. See Appendix A for more comprehensive information than is offered here.
> **bond** A mutual fund whose portfolio consists primarily of bonds.
> **growth** A mutual fund whose portfolio consists of stocks of companies that are expected to increase in value due to rising earnings. It pays

little or no dividends and is suited to the investor who desires appreciation in value rather than current income.

income A mutual fund whose portfolio consists of bonds or high-dividend-paying stocks. It's suited to the investor who desires current income.

load A mutual fund that imposes a sales charge to buy (front-end load) or sell (rear-end load) shares. The load is added to (deducted from) the purchase price (sale proceeds).

money market (also called liquid asset fund or cash fund) A mutual fund that invests in short-term U.S. government and bank securities, bank certificates of deposit, and commercial paper. The net asset value per share of most money market funds is a constant $1.

no-load A mutual fund that does not charge a fee to buy or sell shares.

stock A mutual fund whose portfolio consists of common and preferred stocks.

net asset value The value of all the securities in a mutual fund minus the fund's liabilities divided by the number of shares.

no-fault insurance A state-legislated program that requires that the cost of property damages and personal injuries be paid by each party's insurance company, regardless of who is primarily responsible for the accident.

no-load mutual fund See under **mutual fund.**

non-forfeiture options The options available to a life insurance policy owner who wishes to stop making premium payments but does not want to forfeit the policy. These include using the cash value to pay for (1) term insurance or (2) paid-up life insurance with a smaller death benefit.

policy dividends The return to an insurance policyholder of part of the annual premium. This refund of overpayment results when the insurance company pays out fewer claims than it anticipated.

power of attorney, durable A document authorizing one individual to act as agent on behalf of another individual (the principal) and to manage the principal's affairs if he or she becomes incapacitated.

preferred stock See under **stock.**

premium 1. The annual cost of insurance. 2. The amount by which a bond sells above par value ($1,000).

present value The current worth of an amount to be received in the future, based on the expected rate of compounding. For example, assuming that savings compound at 10% annually, the present value of $10 to be received ten years from now is $3.85 (the result of dividing $10 by the savings factor of 2.594—the intersection of 10% and 10 years on Table 1, page 53).

primary insurance amount The amount of monthly payment to which a worker is entitled upon retirement or disability under the federal Social Security system and the basis for all other benefits.

prime rate   See under **interest.**

principal   1. The face amount of a note, bond, or loan. 2. A person's capital.

probate   The process of admitting a will to court records, deciding questions arising in the administration of an estate, and approving the actions of the executor or administrator of the estate.

property and casualty insurance   See under **insurance.**

prospectus   A document that a company provides for prospective shareholders. It describes management, financial status, and shares to be offered. An investment company (mutual fund) prospectus explains in detail the operations and policies of the fund, its investment objectives (growth stock fund, corporate bond fund, etc.), most recent investments, past performance, fees and commissions, and the procedure for buying and selling shares.

purchasing power risk   The risk that the income and return of principal from an investment will not keep pace with inflation. Investments that pay a fixed rate for a specified period of time (bonds, certificates of deposit) are subject to purchasing power risk because, if prices rise, the return will buy fewer goods and services.

qualified retirement plan   A retirement plan that adheres to the rules and regulations of the Internal Revenue Service. Individual Retirement Accounts, Keogh plans, 401(k) and 403(b) plans, and many company pension plans are qualified. Contributions to a qualified plan are usually tax-deductible, and the earnings within the plan aren't taxed until funds are withdrawn at retirement.

real estate investment trust   See **REIT.**

registered investment advisor   A person who provides investment advice to the public and is required to be registered with the Securities and Exchange Commission. Registration does not imply that the advisor has been sponsored, recommended, or approved by the commission or that his or her abilities or qualifications to act as an investment advisor have been passed upon by the commission.

REIT   An acronym for "real estate investment trust," an investment company that specializes in real estate or mortgage investments. Shares are traded on the major exchanges and are bought and sold like other shares of stock.

rollover   The tax-free transfer of funds from one retirement plan to another. The proceeds of a company pension plan must be transferred to an Individual Retirement Account within sixty days of the date the money becomes available, to qualify as a rollover. Otherwise the amount is subject to tax.

rule of 72   A financial formula that calculates the amount of time it takes an investment to double at a certain rate of interest; the interest rate is divided into 72 (for example, if the rate is 8%, the investment will double in nine years).

savings bond   See under **bond.**

settlement options   The payment choices, other than a lump sum, available to the beneficiary of a life insurance policy. These include (1) monthly payment of interest on the lump sum, (2) payment of the lump sum plus interest over a specified time period, and (3) payment of a certain amount each month until proceeds are used up.

single premium whole life insurance   See under **insurance, life.**

stock   Share of ownership in a corporation; usually implies common stock. See Appendix A for more comprehensive information than given here.
>   **common**   The basic ownership of a corporation. Common stockholders share directly in the success or failure of a business enterprise.
>   **preferred**   A security that entitles the owner to a fixed annual dividend but no participation in the growth of the company's earnings. Price fluctuations are caused by interest rate changes rather than stock market cycles.

stock mutual fund   See under **mutual fund.**

tax-deductible   Expenses that reduce the amount of income subject to income tax. They include mortgage interest, charitable donations, and medical expense.

term insurance   See under **insurance.**

Treasury bond   See under **bond.**

trust   A legal entity that places ownership of property in the name of one person, called the trustee, for the use and benefit of another person.

trustee   A person who holds trust property for the benefit of another.

umbrella liability   See under **insurance, liability.**

Uniform Gift to Minors Act   An act in force in most states that allows irrevocable gifts of property to be made to a minor and held for the benefit of the minor by an adult custodian until the minor reaches majority.

universal life insurance   See under **insurance.**

variable annuity   See under **annuity.**

variable life insurance   See under **insurance, life.**

whole life insurance   See under **insurance, life.**

will   A written document by which a person disposes of property at death. It must conform to certain guidelines in order to be accepted and carried out by the court.

yield, current   The annual return on an investment expressed as a percentage of the current price. If a stock is currently selling at $10 a share and the annual dividend is $1, the stock's current yield is 10% ($1/$10).

yield to maturity   The annualized return on a bond investment, factoring in the gain or loss on the bond when it matures. A bond that is currently selling at a discount from par (less than $1,000) will have a higher yield to maturity than current yield. A bond that's selling at a premium over par (more than $1,000) will have a lower yield to maturity than current yield.

zero coupon bond   See under **bond.**

Recommended Reading

Many of the following books and periodicals can be found at your public library.

Periodicals

Changing Times. The Kiplinger Magazine. General information on personal finance and consumerism.

Modern Maturity. Column on personal finance and articles on financial topics of interest to older individuals.

Money. Financial planning and investments.

Personal Investor. How-to articles on investments and financial topics.

Sylvia Porter's Personal Finance Magazine. Articles on budgeting, taxes, investments, and financial planning.

Books

Donoghue, William E. *William E. Donoghue's Lifetime Financial Planner.* New York: Harper & Row, 1987. Complete do-it-yourself guide to all aspects of financial planning.

———. *William E. Donoghue's No-Load Mutual Fund Guide.* New York: Harper & Row, 1983. Explains the mechanics of investing in mutual funds and their use in financial planning.

Dunnan, Nancy. *Dun & Bradstreet Guide to $Your Investments$.*™ New York: Harper & Row. This annually updated reference guide to investments and financial planning is a must for everyone's bookshelf. In it you will find the answers to every money management question you could possibly think of.

Engel, Louis. *How to Buy Stocks*. Boston: Little, Brown and Co., 1983. Concise advice on the buying and selling of investments, specifically stocks, bonds, and mutual funds.

Hakala, Donald R., and Delaney, Michael M. *Financial Planning for Retirement*. Boston: Allyn and Bacon, Inc., 1983. A comprehensive discussion of important financial considerations, ranging from budgeting to estate planning.

Lister, Harry J., CFP. *Your Guide to IRAs and 14 Other Retirement Plans*. Glenview, IL: Scott, Foresman and Co., 1985. A clearly written, comprehensive guide to retirement plans—how they work, how to make the most of them. Excellent examples and explanations.

Nauheim, Ferd. *The Retirement Money Book*. Washington, DC: Acropolis Books Ltd., 1982. An easy-to-read discussion of a broad range of financial strategies relating to retirement.

Tobias, Andrew. *The Only Other Investment Guide You'll Ever Need*. New York: Simon and Schuster, 1987. Easy-to-read, enjoyable, common-sense approach to investing and financial planning. Paperback.

Vicker, Ray. *The Dow Jones–Irwin Guide to Retirement Planning*. Homewood, IL: Dow Jones–Irwin, 1986. A highly readable book written for the layperson. Identifies key issues of retirement planning through a step-by-step approach.

Pamphlets and Newsletters

Starred (*) booklets are available from: Consumer Information Center–Y, P.O. Box 100, Pueblo, CO 81002.

FEDERAL BENEFITS
"A Brief Explanation of Medicare." An overview of health benefits. Free from your Social Security office.
*"Federal Benefits for Veterans and Dependents." A comprehensive description of benefits with a list of VA facilities nationwide. $1.75.
"Thinking About Retiring?" Deciding when to retire; determining Social Security benefits. Free from your Social Security office.
"A Woman's Guide to Social Security." What women should know about benefits upon retirement, disability, widowhood, and divorce. Free from your Social Security office.
"Your Social Security." All about social security. Free from your Social Security office.

FINANCIAL PLANNING AND INVESTMENTS
*"Alice in Debitland: Consumer Protection and Electronic Banking." Bank cards, automatic teller machines, electronic fund transfer, and protection against theft or computer error. Free.

*"Before You Say Yes: Fifteen Questions to Ask About Investments." Investment advice and protection from fraudulent securities dealers. Free.

*"Money Matters." Tips for selecting a financial planner, accountant, and lawyer. Free.

"Personal Finance." Biweekly newsletter covers specific investment topics. Investor Resource Center provides answers to subscribers' money-related questions. $118 for 24 issues. Personal Finance, P.O. Box 1466, Alexandria, VA 22313-2062.

*"What Every Investor Should Know." Basic information on choosing investments. $1.00.

HEALTH

"Age Pages." Practical health advice for older people. $3.50.

*"Generic Drugs: How Good Are They?" What they are and how they can save you money; the generic names of fourteen commonly prescribed drugs. Free.

"Guide to Health Insurance for People with Medicare." What Medicare pays and doesn't pay; what to look for in private insurance. Free from your Social Security office.

"A Handbook About Care in the Home." A handbook designed to teach older people and their families about home care, the services available, and the agencies that provide them. Free from: AARP Fulfillment, 1090 K Street NW, Washington, DC 20049.

"The Right Place at the Right Time." A guide to long-term care choices for the elderly. Free from: AARP Fulfillment, 1090 K Street NW, Washington, DC 20049.

HOUSING AND HOME EQUITY CONVERSION

Home Equity News. Sample sale/leaseback documents and several publications relating to home equity conversion are available from: National Center for Home Equity Conversion, 110 East Main Street, Room 1010, Madison, WI 53703.

*"Safety for Older Consumers." An extensive checklist for making the home safe for the elderly. 50 cents.

*"Turning Home Equity into Income for Older Homeowners." Explanation of reverse annuity mortgage, sale/leaseback, split equity, and deferred payment loan; costs and risks; consumer safeguards. $1.25.

*"Your Home, Your Choice." Housing options for the elderly. Checklists help you make the right choice. Free.

*"Your Keys to Energy Efficiency." Tips for saving energy at home and in the car. Free.

TAXES

The following publications can be ordered by calling the IRS Publications Office at 1-800-241-3860.

"Comprehensive Tax Guide to U.S. Civil Service Retirement Benefits." Publication 721.

"Credit for the Elderly and the Permanently and Totally Disabled." Publication 524.

"Pension and Annuity Income." Publication 575.

"Tax Information for Older Americans." Publication 554.

"Tax Information on Social Security Benefits." Publication 915.

"U.S. Civil Service Retirement and Disability." Publication 567.

Index